NONFICTION
NOTEBOOKS

NONFICTION NOTEBOOKS

Strategies for Informational Writing

Stenhouse
PUBLISHERS

www.stenhouse.com

Portland, Maine

Aimee Buckner

Stenhouse Publishers
www.stenhouse.com

Credits
Page 92: Figure 5.4: Copyright © 2012 Highlights for Children, Inc., Columbus, Ohio. All rights reserved. Reprinted by permission.

Library of Congress Cataloging-in-Publication Data
Buckner, Aimee E. (Aimee Elizabeth), 1970-
   Nonfiction notebooks : strategies for informational writing / Aimee Buckner. -- Second edition.
      pages cm.
   Includes bibliographical references.
   ISBN 978-1-57110-952-1 (pbk. : alk. paper) -- ISBN 978-1-57110-994-1 (ebook) 1. English language--Composition and exercises--Study and teaching. 2. Exposition (Rhetoric)--Study and teaching. 3. Note-taking--Study and teaching. 4. School notebooks. I. Title.
   LB1576B8828 2013
   372.6--dc23
                                                              2013010387

Cover design, interior design, and typesetting by designboy creative.

Manufactured in the United States of America

For
Mary Baldwin

Contents

Acknowledgments

I would like to express my gratitude to the many teachers, students, colleagues, and friends who pushed me through this work. Writing, for me, is anything but solitary, and your support, encouragement, and advice kept me going.

I would like to thank Philippa Stratton, my editor, for her patience and comments throughout this process. My gratitude goes out to Maureen Barbieri, Mark Overmeyer, and Jennifer Allen for reading and commenting on the different phases of the manuscript. Your comments led me to think deeply and consider different angles for my own teaching as well as writing. In addition, I'd like to thank all of the "behind-the-scenes" people at Stenhouse Publishers, who brought writing from a Word document to a real book I can hold.

Thank you to Brenda Power of Choice Literacy for the writing retreats. I was able to get a lot of work done during those days in Ohio and Maine. Thank you to the colleagues at those retreats—you know who you are—who kept me motivated.

Thank you to Courtney Bean and Courtney Mundt, who invited me into their classrooms and shared their students with me. You are both wonderful teachers, and I learned a lot from working with you. Thank you, also, for reading the manuscript and giving me feedback.

Thank you to all of the students I had the honor of working with at the Lovett School in Atlanta, Georgia, as well as the students in Forsyth County Schools. I couldn't put all of your work in the book, but all of you affected my thinking and teaching. Thank you to the teachers in those schools—I am a better teacher for working with you.

Most importantly, thank you Rick, Samantha, Sydney, and Michael. You didn't complain (much) when dinner was cereal or when I might have forgotten to be somewhere. I love you to the moon and back.

CHAPTER 1

Writer's Notebooks:
An Informational Twist

Notebooks. I have dozens of them now. They're in my basement office stacked in a corner. I look at some from time to time, but overall, the older they are the less I venture through their pages. Some of my notebooks are filled with my childhood memories and memories of my own child growing up. Some are filled with the trials and tribulations of being a single mom, while others have entries focused on former students. It's a hodgepodge of narratives, poetry, snippets of conversations, samples from mentor texts, emails—basically everything that links me to my writing life.

My notebooks make me reflect on what I do as a writer and as a teacher. Sometimes I reflect as I reread, and other times, I reflect when I just look at the stack. I've come a long way from being a nonwriter to a writing teacher who taught writing through January to a true writer. Through this journey, I've changed the way I've used my notebooks. I've adjusted how students use their notebooks. And I've adapted many writing strategies for different genres. This didn't happen overnight and sometimes it didn't happen on purpose. It's been an evolution for me over the years. So, I shouldn't have been surprised when I got this question from a teacher at a conference:

I use notebooks in the beginning of the year for personal narratives, but after that, I don't find notebooks useful. What strategies will work with other genres, or are there separate strategies for different genres?

This is a great question and one that I should keep asking myself. How can my use of a writer's notebook help me write in a variety of ways? I found myself thinking about this question over and over again. It's one that I'm sure a lot of people wonder but don't ask. Or it's one question that you didn't think about, but now that you heard it, you want to know more. This thinking is what led me to write this book. Although I may see the connections between writer's notebooks and various genres, it took me a while to get there. I was one of those teachers who kept the writer's notebook going through the narrative and poetry units and then let it fizzle out. It wasn't that I didn't want the kids writing anymore, but rather I hadn't figured out how to use the notebook in other genres. Now I see the connections, but I realize that it may not be obvious to others—especially my students.

Over the years, as our curriculum has changed to include more genre studies, I've had to rethink and adapt notebook strategies to help my students continue to write fluently. Some strategies I could adapt to several genres, and sometimes my students and I made up new strategies to fit our needs. I kept in mind that the writer's notebook is a tool to help my students develop their ideas, try out different possibilities, and write better first drafts. With that as a guideline, it was easier to see notebook possibilities.

A word about notebooks: Often teachers ask to see the whole process of a piece as it goes through the notebook, into a draft, and out as a finished piece (see Figure 1.1). The writing process doesn't work this way. It's not that neat and orderly. At least it's not for me. The focus of this book is the notebook itself. Students use the notebooks to develop seed ideas and *then again* to support craft and revision. My students create their draft on yellow legal pad paper. Before revisions are made to the draft, students use the notebooks to try out various revisions. Then they transfer changes from the notebook to the draft. Editing and final drafts of student work are not discussed in this book; it's the writer's work in the notebook that is the focus.

Figure 1.1 Notebooks Within the Process

Writer's Tool	Writer's Process	Writer's Work
Writer's Notebook	Gather information, write about seed ideas, find angle, determine audience and mode of writing	• Prewrite • Organize information • Expand the topic
Yellow Legal Pad or Laptop	Draft	• Write first draft • Reread for places to revise
Writer's Notebook	Try out craft and/or revisions	• Draft leads • Draft endings • Draft subheadings • Work on sentence combining • Try out word play
Yellow Legal Pad or Laptop	Revise/edit draft	• Copy what you like from your notebook into the draft (repeat as necessary)

Exploring Ideas

It's nonfiction writing time! It says so in the curriculum calendar, so it must be true. I scramble to get out the graphic organizers, the outline formats, and bunches and bunches of books for research. I'm armed and ready. We'll start with a web to brainstorm. Then we'll move into an outline. Then we'll fill it all in with facts from the books. And hocus-pocus, there will be a report. Sound familiar?

Nonfiction writing is a huge genre. It includes everything from memoir and poetry to informational texts and essays. The Common Core State Standards (CCSS 2012) address the breadth of the nonfiction genre through the way writing expectations are categorized: opinion/argument; informational; and narrative. Informational writing—explanatory writing—is often seen as report writing. Many elementary teachers spend their "nonfiction" unit writing in other subject areas. We have students write a report on an animal or state or battle from the Civil War. As we get more savvy about the different kinds of informational writing, we may even have the kids write an "article" rather than a report. Yet many of those articles sound like reports anyway. Even if we change our wording—like *feature article* instead of *report*—if we don't change our approach to writing, we'll get the same kind of report we've always gotten from our students.

Understanding explanatory writing, the way it works, and how to research topics are key ways to write better material. Many times, as teachers, we don't have the time and maybe not even the inclination to study and learn about informational pieces. What's to know? Nonfiction is based on fact. It's true information. You read some books, write down some facts, make an outline, and, abracadabra, the report comes flying out of a pencil.

The CCSS address this quite clearly with English/Language Arts (ELA)-Literacy-Writing standards 7, 8, and 9 (which include variations appropriate to grade level). Students not only need to be able to read informational texts but also need to use that information to build and present their knowledge of synthesized information. Here are the standards, taken from the fourth-grade page. Note: the research standards are basic and grow more complicated as the grade levels progress. For the purpose of this book, however, I think the fourth-grade versions give us the general idea of what is expected.

Standard 7: Students need to "conduct short research projects that build knowledge through investigation of different aspects of a topic."

This standard scared me at first. Notice the word *projects*—it's plural. That means more than one. What gives me relief is the word *short*. Previously in my teaching, I admit, I may have had my students do one or two large research projects. They lasted weeks, and I was ready to pull my hair out by the end of them. I was also one of those teachers who saved this kind of thing for the end of the year. After some reflection, I realized that this standard gives us the opportunity not only to keep the research short and focused but also to teach these strategies more than once a year.

In addition, standard 7 encourages students to investigate different aspects of the topic. This can be scary, because this means many of us have to change the way we support our student research. Gone are the days that we can give a list of questions for students to answer and on which to base their report. We'll need to find comprehensive research strategies that students can use to approach a topic from different angles.

Standard 8: Students need to "recall relevant information from experiences or gather relevant information from print and digital sources; take notes and categorize information, and provide a list of sources."

I love working with kids, because they find out the most *amazing* information. Unfortunately, these amazing facts are not always relevant to the research at hand. My son had a research project for the 2012 presidential election. Several things had to be included, but in her wisdom, his social studies teacher gave the students a place to write fun facts. So finding out that President Obama has read every Harry Potter book is interesting and fun, but it's not relevant to the election. We can use the same approach by giving students a place to include the fun facts, but also helping them focus on the relevant information they need for their written piece.

Standard 9: Students need to "draw evidence from literary or informational texts to support analysis, reflection, and research."

This is a standard that we've all dealt with. Basically, it asks students to be able to document their research to support their writing. This is where we really need to focus on how to help students "recompose" what they are reading into their own words or graphics that will help them communicate the information without plagiarizing (Moline 2012).

Just as with personal narratives, students will write better if they take the time to develop their thinking and ideas first. This doesn't have to take weeks and weeks. Using what I know about notebooks for supporting personal narratives, I developed strategies to help my students think through nonfiction topics. So instead of just writing down facts about an animal found in Georgia, we first brainstormed topics and problems related to the animal of choice. From there we could determine what we already knew and what we needed to find out. Questions popped up and research became clearer and more concise. Jotting, sketching, and writing in our notebooks helped us think through all the muck to create a clearer vision of what we hoped to write.

Developing a Vision for Writing

When I was growing up, we often wrote reports about the different states. Everyone wanted Hawaii and no one wanted our home state. Stephanie Harvey writes about this same situation in her book *Nonfiction Matters* (1998). Of course, after reading her book, no one wanted to be caught dead assigning a state report. Instead, it seems that teachers assign animal reports. It's fine; I do it too. Kids in elementary school, especially, love animals. Plus, there are many resources readily available for students to use. The classroom magazine *National Geographic Explorer* always has a feature article about an interesting animal or variety of animals. Kids read fiction books starring animals, they write about their pets, and they watch the cable shows on *Animal Planet* and *Discovery Channel*, to name a few. It's a high-interest topic that many kids find engaging.

This is where a notebook can be useful. Whether kids are writing about an animal or something else, a notebook allows them to try out different possibilities for their writing—be it the topic, format, wording, graphics, and so on—before committing to a draft. This is where writers can start to form their vision for a piece. Kids can use different strategies to try out beginnings and endings—just like they do for a narrative piece. They can think about the angle they want to take—perspective. They can think through whether or not their piece will simply be informative or if it will have a persuasive tone. Using a notebook with strategies in mind gives student writers permission to try out different ways of writing before starting the draft.

Students in kindergarten through second grade often write a lot of "all about" books. As students reach the third- through fifth-grade level, we need to build on their ability to use what they know *all about* and help them focus and angle their pieces. Kids need to learn to lift the level of their writing not only through craft but also by having a vision for the kind of writing they want to do, the purpose of their writing, and the audience they intend to reach. As students move into middle school, they need strategies for developing their vision with these ideas in mind as well as weaving narrative into their pieces to further develop their ideas. From trying out different kinds of craft to determining the organization of a piece, using our notebook helps us keep track of all of our attempts—successes and failures. From there we can pick and choose what will go into a draft and what won't.

Writing Better First Drafts

Writing teachers, however, should give careful attention to what happens between the moment the writer receives an idea or an assignment and the moment the first completed draft is begun.

—Donald Murray (1978)

Honestly, I was one of those kids and teachers—who disliked informational writing. I didn't like to read the encyclopedia growing up. I didn't like to research ideas and write things down on note cards. I was the kid who wrote my papers first and designed the outline second. Research bogged me down, and then the whole idea of having to revise just pushed me over the edge. And I wasn't the only one teetering on the revision brink. Many of my students were right there with me. They didn't like to revise because it seemed to them that revision was an acknowledgment that there was something wrong with their work and it needed to be "fixed."

This fight over heavy revisions lasted for years in my classroom. I was always looking for ways to honor rough drafts while helping the student through the revision process so that it wasn't akin to major surgery. Unfortunately, many of these first drafts were, well, awful, and they needed major surgery. Meanwhile, my students remained fiercely committed to their drafts—even if a few changes would instantly improve the piece. Revision remained a battleground.

As I gradually gained experience and insight as a writing teacher, I came to realize that the notebook work we were doing not only helped me plant seed ideas but also grew my writing so that my own first drafts were stronger. And with a stronger first draft, the amount of revision needed was substantially reduced. My energies had been misplaced! Instead of throwing so much energy into the revision stage, I needed to focus on teaching students how to write a *better* first draft so that the revision process ahead would be less painful—for all concerned.

In my classroom, I have found that through the support of notebook work, students can grow their writing and strengthen their ideas. With strong ideas, they can write better first drafts. The work we do in notebooks before rushing into a draft gives us time to envision our work, to find mentor texts we love, and to study those texts. In doing so, we actually are doing a lot of the "revision" on our "vision" before we write the draft. We can use the actual revision process to enhance the writing instead of rewriting large portions of the text.

Students can use their notebooks to plan out the organization, flow, and key ideas of their writing. When kids write a personal narrative, they already know the whole story in their heads—they lived it. When they write "all about" books, kids don't need to do extra research; they spit out all they know about a topic. Once they're out of information, the book ends. As students grow up, their writing needs to become more sophisticated. This means helping them plan out their first draft so it's better than whatever they can just spill out of their heads. This foresight will help students with every kind of writing they'll do.

Genre studies are required in most curriculums. The CCSS suggest that children at various grade levels should be competent with writing opinion/argument pieces, informational/expository pieces, and narrative pieces. Writers need to understand the structure and purpose for the different kinds of writing. Using notebooks, students can explore these kinds of writing separately in genre studies as well as how to combine them to write a more complex text. Through a notebook lens, students will be able to see common threads between these kinds of writing. This foundation is crucial as students continue to live in a world where new kinds of writing are appearing every day. For cxample, when I started teaching school, we didn't have e-mail. When we got e-mail, we weren't publishing class websites or blogs. Now that we're publishing websites and blogs, we're finding we can have study groups online, write on wiki pages, keep notes on electronic white-boards that save to the computer, keep online notebooks, give feedback to other posts, and even create applications to make our work easier. It's crazy fun for writers everywhere—even for people who don't realize they're "writing." So, arming students with strategies to approach new (and old) ways of writing will give them the confidence they'll need to write into the future.

A Notebook Bonus

Just like the infomercials that keep saying "but there's more," there is a bonus to expanding writer's notebooks to all the genres your students will study. The writer's notebook is the ideal place for a student to grow toward being an independent writer. The notebook establishes a place and habit of mind for students to write often and explore a topic no matter what the genre. As students take more ownership —become more independent with their notebook writing—they will be able to keep these habits of mind throughout their writing life, not just for a unit in the fourth grade. And while students are writing in their note-books, the teacher has time to confer and teach students individually to make good decisions about their own writing.

As students become independent writers, they make choices not only about their topic but also about the genre in which they'll write, the form of their writing, the purpose and audience for their writing, and the mentor texts they'll study. Using notebook strategies to think through information, students can move from writing according to the teacher's vision (or the state's vision) to writing according to their *own* vision. When students have a notebook and strategies to approach a new genre or format of writing, there is nothing they won't be able to write—today or in the future. Considering there are forms of writing yet to be invented, we owe it to our students to teach them in a way that will set them up for inventing their tomorrow.

A Word About the Workshop Format

I'm finding that more and more teachers are using the language of the writing workshop, but we may apply this language differently. For the purpose of this book, a writing workshop is about forty-five to sixty minutes each day. It starts with a five-minute mini-lesson, which connects the previous day's lesson (or something the children already know how to do) to the current lesson. This is usually a whole-class lesson that includes a minute or two to try out the work at hand. Then the work of the workshop begins. Students move off to work on their individual writing projects. Kids may work independently, with writing partners, or even within a small group. The teacher may work with a small group, a set of writing partners, or confer individually. The individual conferences are key to student growth, not an afterthought. The class time wraps up with a share session. During these last five minutes or so, the teacher may recap the day's lesson and how he or she observed students implementing it in their writing. Or a teacher may choose a student or two to share some of their writing. Finally, the teacher sets up the next day's work by discussing how today's work will help them be better writers tomorrow.

This is a brief overview of the workshop structure that I use. I know teachers may tweak the workshop to fit their busy schedules or to meet the requirements of their building principals. But, as you read this book, know that this is the format within which I worked. For more thorough explanations, you can refer to the following:

The Art of Teaching Writing; Units of Study for Primary Writing; and *Units of Study for Teaching Writing, Grades 3–5* by Lucy Calkins

Writing Workshop: The Essential Guide by Ralph Fletcher and JoAnn Portalupi

The Writing Workshop: Working Through the Hard Parts (And They're All Hard Parts) by Katie Wood Ray and Lester Laminack

CHAPTER 2

Strategies to Explore Topics

Writers need to understand the various text structures available within a genre. Writers also must learn to think of themselves as readers, understanding how to get their meaning across by practicing comprehension strategies. This reading-writing link is essential in building a strong foundation from which students will write.

Whenever I move classrooms, I spend a couple of days walking around my boxes, unpacking and sifting through things. I need to get a feel for the room before I organize it, arrange it, and finally set it up so it's ready for children. I need time to visualize workspace, storage, and flow. I walk around the school, peeking in other teachers' classrooms. I look at their desk arrangements, where their classroom libraries are located, where they plan to pull large and small groups. When I think I'm ready, I begin sketching in a notebook. I work and rework different arrangements until I think I finally have a plan—a vision of what my classroom will look like that year. This can take me as little as a few days to as long as the whole summer. And of course, I revise throughout the year. It's this kind of process I lead my students through as they encounter new kinds of writing.

Before the first day of our informational writing unit of study, I spend time during our reading workshop immersing my students in different kinds of informational texts. In order to write this genre, students need to know how to read its various kinds of texts. While reading aloud, I'm careful to use the same kind of intonation and pacing I might use with a narrative text. I slow down when I want to create some suspense. I speed up my reading when it seems to be exciting. I chunk the words into phrases that will help students understand and visualize what I'm reading. This modeling is important at all grade levels. As the text gets more difficult to read, as it likely will do with informational books, students do not always get punctuation cues for intonation and phrasing. We have to help them with that. After I've modeled reading this genre for the whole class, I phase students into informational books for their individual reading, small groups, or book clubs.

As students read a variety of texts in this genre, they'll find there are many different organizational structures (see Figure 2.1). These structures will affect how a student writes and how a reader reads. Recognizing and understanding the different text structures will help writers make better decisions with regard to how to write about their topic and how best to organize their work for their reader.

Students need to understand that they will use the same comprehension strategies with informational texts as they have used with narrative texts. This may mean reviewing how these strategies help readers of inconsiderate texts—texts that don't have an interesting topic or are not written in a kid friendly way. Reminding students of tools that they already know how to use will help them grapple with new and different kinds of reading. In turn, it will open students up to new and different ways of writing about what may seem like old topics.

As students read and/or listen to informational texts, it's important for them not only to be aware of the comprehension strategies they're using but also to learn how to make note of their new understanding without plagiarizing. Steve Moline discusses recomposing in his book *I See What You Mean: Visual Literacy K-8, Second Edition*: "Recomposing is simply reading information in one format and summarizing it in another format" (2012, 29). So, if students are practicing visualizing text that has no pictures, they may take notes in the form of a sketch or a diagram.

I love starting off a unit of study by reminding my students to visualize with informational text. Although many books and magazines have pictures and diagrams, kids sometimes skip them—especially as they get into the upper grades. It's important that students not only look at the pictures and graphics but add on to them as they read. *Exploding Ants: Amazing Facts About How Animals Adapt* by Joanne Settel (1999) has short, two-page expository articles about different animals and their adaptations. I read aloud several of these—without show-

Figure 2.1 Text Structures Students Might Encounter with Informational Reading

Text Structure/ Organization	What It Looks Like	Cue Words	Where to Find It
Chronological or Sequence	Presents facts or events in order of occurrence; can be organized by time or by steps in a process	*first, second, third, then, next, before, after, last, finally*	history books, biographies, diaries/ journals; *Snowflake Bentley* (Martin 2009)
Cause and Effect	Presents information to help the reader understand what caused an event to occur	*if, so, so that, because, since, in order to*	*Thank You, Sarah: The Woman Who Saved Thanksgiving* (Anderson 2002) *If You Give a Mouse a Cookie* (Numeroff 1985) *The Doorbell Rang* (Hutchins 1986) *Tornadoes* (Simon 1999) *Liberty! How the Revolutionary War Began* (Penner 2002)
Compare and Contrast	Presents information by similarities and/ or differences among people, concepts, events, etc.	*the same as, unlike, alike, compared to, resembles, yet, but*	*George vs. George: The American Revolution as Seen from Both Sides* (Schanzer 2004) Who Would Win? series (Pallotta) *I Am the Dog, I Am the Cat.* (Hall 1994)
Problem and Solution	Presents information to demonstrate a problem and its solution	*problem, solution, because, since, so that*	*A River Ran Wild* (Cherry 2013)

Note: There are many other organizational patterns, including but not limited to description, spatial, definition/example, and classification. The table describes some of the more common kinds of organizational structures I have found in my research for this book and for my own teaching. I recommend reading "Teaching Expository Text Structures Through Informational Trade Book Retellings" (Moss 2004). A quick Google search will bring up several websites with information as well.

ing students the pictures—to help them visualize the text. Following Steve Moline's concept of recomposing, I ask the students to sketch what they see in their mind's eye and use labels or captions to help them remember what they are learning. I also use Stephanie Harvey and Anne Goudvis's *Toolkit Texts* (2007), which focuses on the use of short nonfiction articles. Other favorite resources for read-alouds and mini-lessons include *National Geographic Explorer* classroom magazine, *Ranger Rick*, and *Highlights for Children*. (See Figure 2.2 for examples of texts and lessons to immerse students with informational text outside of social studies and science class.)

Figure 2.2 Ideas for Read-Alouds and Mini-Lessons Focused on Informational Texts

Excerpt/Book	Resource/Author	Mini-Lessons
"Living Honey Jars"	*Exploding Ants: Amazing Facts About How Animals Adapt* by Joanne Settel (1999)	Visualizing Determining importance Using fix-up strategies
"Arachnids All Around"	*The Tarantula Scientist* by Sy Montgomery (2004)	Asking questions Making inferences Using fix-up strategies
"Far-Out Foods"	*National Geographic Explorer* by Diane Wedner (2010)	Determining importance Synthesizing
Never Smile at a Monkey: And 17 Other Important Things to Remember	By Steve Jenkins (2009)	Asking questions Determining importance Making inferences
How They Croaked: The Awful Ends of the Awfully Famous	By Georgia Bragg (2012)	Asking questions Synthesizing Visualizing

To promote the reading and writing of informational text, build a solid informational section in your classroom library. Take care to categorize them by topic, author, and levels—as you would with your narrative books—to help students navigate through the wide variety of books available. I also have a section in my library that has pairs of fiction and informational books. (See Figure 2.3 for examples.) All of this "reading work" sets up the students to write better informational texts. It prepares them to read and understand the research they'll need to do. It prepares them to be able to read as a reader and then as a writer. It prepares them to blend ideas and angles other authors have used to make their writing unique.

Figure 2.3 Fiction/Narrative and Informational Text Pairs

Fiction/Narrative	Informational
Little House on the Prairie by Laura Ingalls Wilder (2010; 75th anniversary edition)	*If You Traveled West in a Covered Wagon* by Ellen Levine (1992)
Shark Tooth Tale; Ready, Freddy! series by Abby Klein (2006)	*Amazing Sharks!* (I Can Read Level 2) by Sarah L. Thomson (2006)
The Gadget War by Betsy Duffey (2000)	*Odd Boy Out: Young Albert Einstein* by Don Brown (2008)
Riding Freedom by Pam Muñoz Ryan (1998)	*The Secret Soldier: The Story of Deborah Sampson* by Ann McGovern (1990)

From Reading to Writing

On the first day of our informational writing session, I gather students around the easel for our mini-lesson. Students sit in front of me on beanbag chairs, large pillows, or small chairs and open their notebooks to the next clean page.

Before I can start, George raises his hand and says, "There isn't anything on the chart paper today."

"I know," I say.

"You usually have what writers do on it. You know, like *writers think about drawing a picture with words,* or something like that," he continues.

"You're right, George. Today, we're going to figure out what writers do and *then* write it on our chart paper."

"Huh?" He looks at me with his freckled face squished up like he smells a rat.

"Today we are going to read. Writers read a lot before they write. We've been reading a lot of different informational texts in our reading workshop, and we've focused on what readers do to understand the text better. Today, we're going to read like writers to see how writers go about writing informational text. On your tables [groups of desks] I have put a big pile of books."

The children all start to stretch their necks and twist around to see these stacks. This cracks me up, because they were just at their seats when I put the books out there.

"Over the next day or two, we're going to use our writing time to *read* different kinds of informational writing," I continue.

"We're reading instead of writing?" George wants clarification.

"Yes. But we're reading as writers. I want you to stop for a few minutes after each book or article or poem you read and think about what the author did to make the topic interesting or different from other nonfiction books you've read. Jot your thinking in your notebook, and we'll meet back here to share our findings."

As the kids head off to find something to read, George stops at the easel and asks, "Can I write something on the chart paper?"

"Sure," I reply, giving him a marker.

Writers read, he writes. "That's better," he says as he moves off to get his books.

A Note About the Stacks of Books on the Kids' Tables

The students have been reading informational texts in reading workshop for a week or two by now. During this time, I've noted the kinds of books the children are choosing to read. I've noticed not only the topics they seem to like but also the structures and organization of the texts they're choosing.

I have about twenty to twenty-five books on each table for four to five children. There are a variety of topics that my students enjoy. Many of the books or articles are familiar to them and some are new. I've made sure to have some easy books, some books at about their reading level, and some slightly challenging books in each stack. I want students to be successful at examining the writing of each book, so I'm not worried about challenging them as readers at this moment.

Strategy: They Did What? (Noticing What Writers Do)

Writers do read, and when it comes to narrative writing, I don't always feel like I have to take writing time for the kids to read more narratives. Informational writing is different. There are a ton of topics and a variety of formats writers can use. In order for my students to get a sense of all the different topics and ways they can write, they need to take time to read.

Within a few minutes of my students reading informational texts, the first hand goes up. "Ms. Buckner, what are we supposed to write in our notebooks?"

I walk over to talk with Emma, who asked the question. "What did you read, Emma?"

"I read an article in *National Geographic Kids* about this guy who eats bugs. It was gross," she says.

"What do you mean gross? How did the author gross you out?" I ask.

"Well, her subheading said 'Sweet Snack,' so I thought it was about candy. Then I read it, and it was about honey ants that people actually *eat*," she says.

"So the writer's subheading got you interested because you thought it was about candy, and then she really wrote about eating bugs. Right?" I summarize what she said.

"Yup."

"That's what you write in your notebook. Just like that. It's really a great observation."

I begin to move around the classroom, answer similar questions, and help students summarize their thinking and notice how the author wrote. Students stay engaged with reading and writing throughout our work time.

As I look around I see that students have different ways of collecting their observations about informational writing. (See samples that follow.) Some are writing a sentence or two after they read the book or article. Some students make a list of things the writer did. It doesn't matter to me how they write about what they notice; it matters that they notice things about the writing.

Emma's notebook:

I like how the book *The True or False Book of Horses* (by Patricia Lauber) has a true or false question but not the answer right away. You have to read the information on the page to know whether the statement is true or false.

Evan's notebook:

Who Would Win? Polar Bear vs. Grizzly Bear (by Jerry Pallotta)
This book compares two bears. On one side is the stuff about polar bears and the other side is about grizzly bears. He also uses a dash—to include examples. "These colors allow grizzlies to blend in with their environment—fallen leaves, dirt, rocks, and trees." (p9)

Connor's notebook:

"Have a Toga Party" by Marcia Amidon Lusted

- seems like author is talking to me
- has drawings with talking bubbles (fiction in nonfiction?)
- the purple sentences break up the piece—main ideas?
- uses words like: first, next, now—to show you what to do

As we come back to the group, the kids are buzzing with what they read.

"What did you notice?" I begin.

Robert speaks up. "The books were on different topics."

"There weren't just books. There were magazines too," says Emma.

"I found a poster folded up in our pile," Michelle pipes into the conversation.

"Okay, so we noticed two things: When writers read, they notice the topics other writers choose." I write *Different topics* on the chart paper. "They also notice that there are different ways to publish a piece—like a book, article, or even a poster." I write *Different kinds of writing.*

Camille raises her hand. "I noticed that sometimes a book had true or false questions and sometimes it just had subheadings."

"Mine was comparing and contrasting bears," says George.

"I think mine was a 'how to' kind of article," Emma adds.

"Excellent. Those are different ways to organize the text. We'll be talking about other ways books are organized, but for now I'll add it to our chart." I write *Organization styles.*

Our conversation continues as kids add to the list to include vocabulary, different styles and amounts of text, pictures, graphs, and so on. "Boys and girls, writers notice all of these things when they're about to dive into a different kind of writing. We're going to work on informational pieces, but as writers, you have some decisions to make. Tomorrow we'll continue reading, but we'll also start exploring what topics interest you." We wrap up our session with George wanting to add on to the top of the chart: *Writers read . . . and notice.* I couldn't say it better myself.

Strategy: Topic Logs

When we gathered for our share time on that first day of our informational writing unit, students were able to share the different topics they read about in books and magazines. They noticed different formats of books, and they began to envision what they wanted to do in their writing. This is the starting point for informational writing. As they're getting jazzed about all the things they might write about, it is time to get them into their notebooks to figure out how to determine their own topic. We dove into this the next day.

"Boys and girls, you're reading a lot of informational pieces. As we said yesterday, there are a lot of topics out there—and many, many different ways in which to write about them. Today, we're going to think about what topic might work well for you."

I turn to my chart paper, where this statement is written: *Writers think about the different angles from which they can write about the same topic.*

I show them a diagram that looks a bit like this:

Inside the box, I write a topic that I know a lot about: *The Endurance.*

"Boys and girls, I have a topic I know a lot about; it's a ship called the *Endurance.* It was built to travel through the Southern Ocean to reach Antarctica. A 'southern' ocean may sound warm, but it isn't. This ocean has cold, icy waters. The ship had to be strong enough to withstand the pressure of the ice packs and any icebergs it might encounter, but it wasn't. The ship was crushed. Crushed by the ocean freezing over. The ice squeezed so hard against the ship that it broke apart and sank. I might want to write about it."

"Was it like the *Titanic*?" asks Emma.

"Well, unlike on the *Titanic*, everyone on the ship survived," I say. "So I can grow a leg to my topic and write at the foot of it: *survivors.* Maybe I'll write about how everyone survives."

"You could compare the ship to the *Titanic*," says George.

"You're right," I say. I draw another leg and write *Titanic* at the foot. "I could also focus on one of the people who were on board. There was a captain, a photographer, a doctor, and a bunch of men on the crew."

"You could write *people* at the end of another leg," volunteers Emma.

"I could, but I want to be more specific. Instead of people I want to write about one person. I'll write *Ernest Shackleton, captain*," I say. After writing this third leg, I invite the children to try this in their notebooks.

"Boys and girls, let's take a few moments to think about all the things you already know a lot about. Remember our list and star strategy? We make a list of things and then put a star by the ones we want to write more about. Today, let's jot a quick list—an expert list. What do you know a lot about? If I had a question about, hmm, horses, who could answer it?"

Sydney raises her hand. "I know a ton about horses!"

"Okay, so on Sydney's expert list, she can put *horses.* Turn to your partner and take a moment to talk about the things you are an expert on." After a couple of minutes I pull their attention back to me.

"It sounds like you all have several things to put on a list. Go ahead and jot them down now."

"And star everything, because you know you can write about them," adds George. (What would I do without him?)

Once most students have three or four ideas down, I direct them to put the topics in boxes on a clean page of their notebooks.

The children start making boxes and writing a word in each box. I remind them to leave a little room between each box for legs that will grow. Some students fit two boxes on a page, others three or four. After a moment or two, I ask the kids to popcorn share—everyone shares one word out loud without being called on, but not at the same time. "Choose one of the topics you wrote down, and we'll do a popcorn share. I'll start: baseball." Students begin slowly at first, but eventually everyone shares a topic: dogs, comics, football, dancing, cookies, books, frogs, and so on.

"Good job," I say. "If you heard a topic that you also know a lot about, you can write that in a box too. Otherwise, try to come up with a couple more topic boxes." After another minute or so, I stop the students. "Okay. Read over your topics. You know a lot about these, right?" The children nod their heads affirmatively. "Okay, now you'll do some writer's work: you're going to think about the smaller topics within these big ones. Grow a leg for each small topic you think of. You might have more than three or you might only have two. Get started."

"For all of them?" asks Fritz.

"For as many of them as you can," I reply. This is the point where students and I will be able to tell which topics they really do know a lot about and which ones may peter out quickly in their writing. It can also help identify topics kids want to know more about, which is okay too.

Without much hesitation at all, the children start drawing their legs and jotting down their topics (see Figure 2.4). This is a strategy in which kids are doing a lot of writerly work without knowing they're doing it. They are narrowing down their topic—discovering which topics may provide slim pickings or not enough to sustain a whole writing piece. It also helps students reflect on topics that they are interested in and they know a little bit about it, but on which

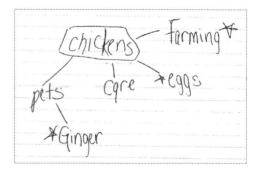

Figure 2.4 Towner uses the "topic legs" strategy.

they'll need to do more research. All of this goes into their thinking as they consider the writing possibilities before they decide on a final selection. All of this work is important for writers to do, and yet it can be overwhelming for students. Sometimes kids skip this kind of prewriting and just choose a topic without considering if it's too big or not big enough. Taking the time to do this "topic legs" strategy encourages students to think about all the possibilities they have as a writer in order to make a topic choice they can live with and enjoy through the writing process.

"Okay, who would like to tell us about their topic legs?" I ask.

Towner volunteers. "In my box I put *chickens*. Then I grew a bunch of legs. I put each of my chickens at the end of the legs: *Clara, Ginger, Marshall,* and *George*." He looks at our George and smiles. "I also have a leg that says *hawk*, because Ginger was eaten by a hawk. I have other legs that say *eggs, chicken coop,* and *taking care of chickens*. I might write a how-to-take-care-of-chickens article."

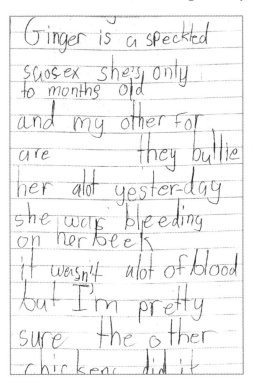

"Good job, Towner. I like how you kept putting legs on your topic as you thought about the smaller pieces. You didn't put all your eggs in one basket." (Students groan at that.)

Many of my students love the "topic legs" strategy. It gives them permission to think about their topic from different angles—from different perspectives. After the students finish working through their topics and growing legs, they can begin an entry using the idea on the foot of each leg. (See Figures 2.5 and 2.6.)

Figure 2.5 Towner wrote this entry about one chicken, Ginger, after using the "topic legs" strategy.

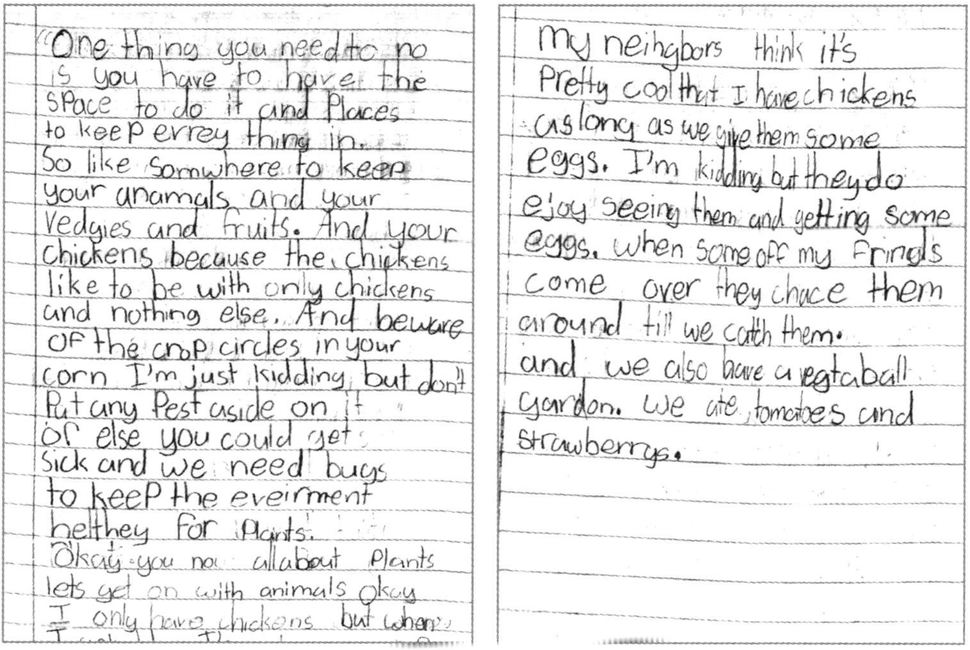

One thing you need to no
is you have to have the
space to do it and Places
to keep errey thing in.
So like somwhere to keep
your anamals and your
Vedgies and fruits. And your
Chickens because the chickens
like to be with only chickens
and nothing else. And beware
of the crop circles in your
corn I'm just kidding but don't
Put any Pest aside on it
or else you could get
sick and we need bugs
to keep the everiment
helthey for Plants.
Okay you now all about Plants
lets get on with animals okay
I only have chickens but when

my neihgbors think it's
Pretty cool that I have chickens
as long as we give them some
eggs. I'm kidding but they do
ejoy seeing them and getting some
eggs. when some off my Frings
come over they chace them
around till we catth them.
and we also have a vegtaball
gardon. We ate tomatoes and
strawberrys.

Figure 2.6 Towner's entry about farming came from his topic legs, but it shows a very different approach than writing about a specific chicken. Giving students time to explore the different angles of a topic helps them develop their vision for the final piece.

Strategy: Take a Tour

Museums are fascinating. You can see all kinds of interesting things. And that's part of the beauty; they are buildings filled with . . . things. Whether it's an art museum, a science museum, or a history museum, the exhibits are created to highlight a different topic. We walk through museums learning about a lot of different things or stay in one or two exhibits to study one or two ideas of interest.

When students are grappling with what to write about for an informational piece, it's interesting to have them make a museum exhibit—in their notebook—on a topic. I start this lesson by sharing the beginning of *Escape! The Story of the Great Houdini* by Sid Fleischman:

> *Not long ago the breast pocket snipped from a man's pajamas came up for auction in New York City. Immediately, bids around the room*

erupted like doves flushed from cover. So eager was the crowd for this fragment of sleepwear that a lofty price of $3,910 was reached before the auctioneer banged his hammer and shouted, "Sold!"

Why would anyone want the pocket of an old pair of striped pajamas with the initials **HH** *monogrammed in gray?*

Easy. The first initial stood for Harry. The second for Houdini.

Harry Houdini, *the world's greatest magician and escape artist. No jail cell, no chains, no manacles could hold the man.*

Houdini, *who walked through a red-brick wall! He came through without a scratch, too.*

Houdini, *who clapped his hands like cymbals and made a five-ton elephant disappear into thin air. Not even the elephant knew how he did it.* (2006, 1)

"Boys and girls, when I first read this, I thought to myself, the pajama pocket is just the kind of thing that would be in a museum. It might even have a little card that said: Harry Houdini's pj pocket—sold for $3,910."

The children nod in agreement.

"I then wondered, hmm, what else might be in a room of a museum dedicated to The Great Houdini? Maybe his magic hat or the box he could cut in half. Maybe they would have the chains he was wrapped in and then broke out of without a key. Maybe, just maybe, they would have a brick from the wall he walked through. It makes me wonder."

I open my notebook. "You know, writers can create anything they want. They can even create a museum exhibit in their notebook. I'm writing an informational piece about the ship, the *Endurance*, right now. If I were to create an exhibit about this ship . . .," I pause to think (and for effect), then say, ". . . I would have the captain's log—the book he kept about what happened—in the museum." In my notebook, I write *captain's log*. I continue, "I might even have a picture of the crew or one of the actual life boats from the ship." I stop to jot these down.

George raises his hand. "If I had a museum about dogs, I'd have paw prints everywhere so people could see how big and how small dogs can be."

"That is exactly the kind of thing you should write down, George. Boys and girls, sometimes writers think about the 'things' that are important to their topics. If you're writing about being a quarterback, your list might include a football or a helmet. If you're writing about a place like your summer camp then you might have a bunk bed or a rope swing. If you're writing about a machine—like airplanes—you might have parts of it in your exhibit.

"Writers think about this, because it helps them focus their topic. Today, I want you to try this for one or more of the topics you're considering for your informational piece. If you have a hard time with one topic, try a different one."

Note: Some students will need to build up their knowledge to complete this strategy. That's fine; they can do some reading and then try the strategy. In the next chapter, I address strategies for helping students build their knowledge base for their selected topic.

Strategy: At the Heart of It

After a few months of writing this book, I went on a writing retreat with my friend Brenda. I had told Brenda I was writing a ton and sent her some of the work.

"You only sent me fifteen pages," she said.

"What? That chapter felt like writing fifty pages at least," I laughed, but I was serious.

I thought a lot about this little snippet of information. I spent a few weeks working on that chapter, and it really did feel like it should be longer than fifteen pages. As I reread the work, I realized my writing was all over the place. Brenda might have thought that this was the entire book. What a mess. I realized that I didn't have a strong main idea for that chapter. I had to sit down and think, what was at the heart of what I was trying to say? What was my focus?

The same thing happens to students, especially if they are overwhelmed by their topic. Helping students figure out what they actually want to say can clear the way to a stronger, more focused piece. This strategy, "at the heart of it," is a twist on Georgia Heard's heart mapping, described in her book *Awakening the Heart: Exploring Poetry in Elementary and Middle School* (1998). Instead of having students think of all the things they hold dear to their heart in order to find a topic, I have them focus just on their topic. I want them to think of what's most important about the piece they are going to write. This helps them determine not only the main idea but also the angle from which they may choose to write their piece.

"Boys and girls, I'd like you to open your notebook to the next clean page. On this page, I want you to draw an outline of a large heart. Take up the whole page for this."

"We did this before," says Towner.

"You're right. We did this in the beginning of the year to find out what was important to you. But remember, writers use strategies over and over again with different topics. Today, we'll use the heart to help us focus our information pieces."

After everyone has drawn their hearts, I instruct them to write their informational topic in the middle. I write: *the* Endurance.

"Last time we used this strategy," I say, "we found out about all the things that were important to *you*. Today, we'll use the same strategy to find out what you think is important for other people to know about your topic. What do you want to say to your readers?"

I turn my attention to the heart I'd drawn. "I'm writing about the *Endurance*. I want people to know that everyone survived. So I'll write *everyone lives*. I also want my readers to know that, to save his crew, Ernest Shackleton gave up his dream of leading his expedition to cross Antarctica from one coast of the continent through the South Pole and to the other coast. I'll write *Shackleton saves men*. Notice that I'm just writing some phrases. It was really cold and they had a dangerous journey. So I'll also write some notes about that. Maybe . . . *climbed mountains, sailed rough seas, walked on ice*." I jot these phrases around my heart.

"Can we draw?" Towner asks.

"You can put a few sketches. You might want to label them. Take a few minutes to think about what's important for others to know about your topic and write those things down in and around your heart." (See Figure 2.7.)

After a few minutes, I ask the students to stop their work and share with a partner. "Okay," I say, "now that you have some ideas, you can read your heart to your partner. Then, think to yourself, If I had to choose one *big* idea to tell my reader—an idea that would summarize this heart—what would it be? Talk with your partner to figure out what that summary sentence would sound like. You'll then write it down in your notebook under your heart (see Figure 2.8). For example, I might write: *Ernest Shackleton did amazing things to save his men.* I could also write: *The* Endurance *and the* Titanic *were both sunk by ice, but their passengers had very different experiences.* I write the first statement below my heart.

"Wait," says Camille. "You said your topic was the *Endurance,* not Ernest Shackleton."

"Yes," Robert says, "but Ernest Shackleton was the captain of the ship."

I explain, "You might find that your main idea is connected to your topic but focuses on a different part of it. My main idea focuses on the captain rather than the whole ship or its journey."

"You have two main ideas," observes Emma. "They don't really go together."

"Actually, they're connected. Like Robert pointed out, I realize the story of the ship isn't as interesting to me as Ernest Shackleton. But it will be impossible for me to write about

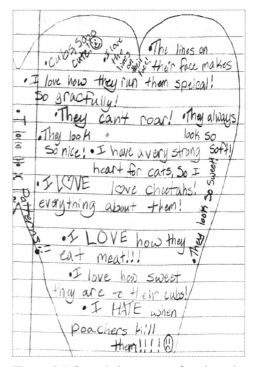

Figure 2.7 Penny's heart map for cheetahs shows how much she loves the cuddly look of a cheetah. Yet at the bottom, she explodes with "I HATE when poachers kill them!!!!" She is grappling with the idea that people intentionally kill this beautiful animal. Her piece may focus on why poachers need to be stopped.

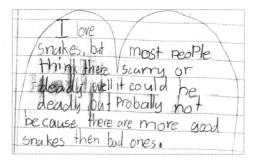

Figure 2.8 From reading Towner's heart map about snakes, we see that he can lift the main idea for his informational piece: Although there are poisonous snakes, most snakes are harmless.

Shackleton without telling the story of the *Endurance*. My main idea has shifted to a different angle—focusing on Ernest Shackleton and not the ship itself. Once you decide on your main idea, you can work in your notebook to develop it."

Strategy: Connect P3

I used to love connect-the-dots activities—drawing line segments between different numbered points to create a picture. I loved them, in part, because I was not the most talented artist. I had a difficult time envisioning how to actually draw something. Then, in college, an art professor told me to draw the negative space—to think of the shapes around the object and draw that. Finally, I had a way to begin drawing without the dots.

Connecting dots to make a big picture is a useful metaphor for writers. We often have to think of the many connections to our topic in order to see the big picture. As we know from reading comprehension strategies (Harvey and Goudvis 2007), making connections is one way we come to understand something more deeply.

For this strategy, I ask students to think about the different kinds of connections we make as readers: text to self, text to text, and text to world, to name a few. The number of connections we make can be infinite as our understanding increases.

"Boys and girls, one thing I do as a writer is I think like a reader. I use the comprehension strategy "making connections" to think about my topic more deeply. For example, I may write about dogs," I say. I show the students my notebook, where I've written the word *dogs* in the center of a page. "Dogs is a big topic," I continue. "So I'm going to try to think of all the people, places, and problems that are connected to dogs."

I begin making a web around the word *dogs*. I write: *training, neighbors, basement, shelter,* and *fighting*. I stop and show my students. "I can probably write some more, but I want to show you the next step. Some of these connections are connected to each other. For example, *training* and *basement* are connected, because we had to train our dog not to go in the basement. I can also connect *neighbors* and *training*, because my neighbors are training their dog to fetch the paper in the morning. Each day we see them out there with their coffee, telling Clarie to fetch. When she does, they give her a treat."

"What about fighting?" Robert asks. "What's the connection there?"

"Well, dog fighting is a problem. Some people actually want dogs to fight. I think this is cruel, and a lot of people are trying to stop it from happening. Unlike the other topics, this is something outside of my own experience. I'll have to research that more.

"Think about one of the topics you're exploring for your informational piece. Jot it in the middle of your page. Spend two minutes thinking about all the people, places, and problems that are connected to it."

The students begin writing. Some get the hang of it more quickly than others. About a minute into the writing I say, "Take a moment to turn and talk to your partner. Tell them quickly three connections you've made. Then go back to writing more connections."

When students turn and talk with a partner or popcorn share, it's a quick way for them not only to share their thinking but also to hear other ideas. These ideas may spark other ideas for their own writing. It's misleading to think that writers write in isolation. Sometimes they do, but they actually talk about their writing a lot. When I'm working on a book or an article, I often post something on Facebook to see what other people are thinking about the idea. I also talk to my editors or close friends to flesh out my ideas. Sometimes I just listen to other teachers talk about their own experiences—even if they have nothing to do with what I'm writing about. Sometimes, I can draw on these conversations to move my thinking forward. So, it is important to give students time throughout the writing process to talk through what they're thinking, to read aloud what they're writing, and to hear how other students are approaching their writing work.

After two minutes have passed, I stop the students. "Now, take one minute to draw lines between the connections that also connect—just like I connected *neighbors* to *training*." Again, students reread their work and begin connecting their ideas. "Now, writers, you can really work this strategy by generating some notebook entries about these connections. You may have just a little bit to write for some of them, but for other connections you'll have more energy and you'll write more. And there will be some where you'll realize that you need to do more research before you can write more."

* * *

It's important to note that students may not need to use all of the strategies discussed in this chapter each time they write an informational piece. As teachers, we need to be mindful of what our students need and how much of it they need at a certain point in time. Sometimes, in my excitement for starting a new writing project, I spend too much time mining my topics. So much so that I'm tired of my topic before I even write the draft. As teachers, we need to manage the energy level of our students, teaching them enough strategies to help them develop their topics, but not so many at one time that they're exhausted before the first draft. If we have several short research projects throughout the year, as suggested by standard 7 of the CCSS, then there is plenty of time to review and introduce strategies to strengthen our students' writing.

CHAPTER 3

Strategies to Gather Information

Last spring, I went to a writing workshop to work on a children's book. It was there that I finally figured out how to research effectively without being overwhelmed. I was writing a story about a duck, and one of my colleagues asked me if everything I said about the duck was true. She wasn't asking whether the duck was real but rather whether the duck was, well, duck-like. I hadn't thought about that. What's there to know about ducks? I opened my notebook and jotted down what I didn't know but needed to know about ducks. From there I was able to determine a couple of research questions and launch myself on a duck-fact hunt. Over the course of two days—on and off—I talked with experts, researched websites, and read a couple of quick articles that would help me with my questions. Because of this, I was able to find some inaccuracies in my stories. For instance, ducks don't have the sense of smell. I didn't know that, and in my story the duck smelled donuts. *Can't happen.* I was able to revise that part of my book to be more accurate.

Using this experience, I now understand that kids do not need to research what they already know. They need to research what they don't know yet. If your students are like mine, they may not understand what they don't know. So they also need to confirm whether or not their own knowledge is accurate, like I did with the duck's sense of smell. Going through a "confirmation process" allows students not only to confirm what they know but also to form new questions about what they really don't know.

This may sound obvious, but how many times have we seen kids do an animal report and research the habitat and what the animal eats, when they know darn well that owls live in forests and eat mice? I'm now wondering how many kids are bored with research because they're actually researching things they already know just to have a resource. Also, students' informational writing experiences in the early grades are primarily with "all about" books, where they rely on a variety of facts that they already know to write a book about a topic they love. By third grade, it's time to lift the level of that writing—from "all about" to angled and focused pieces. The following strategies direct students to find information that's new to them, take notes, and avoid plagiarism.

Strategy: All About

I have yet to meet a kid who doesn't like to know it all. As a matter of fact, I sometimes find it frustrating when my students are so desperate to be right that they can't admit to themselves that there may be more to know about a topic. Many times it's my stronger writers who are the hardest to convince that there is more to know.

"Boys and girls," I begin, "today we are going to do what writers do before they start to research." I read the title on my chart paper to the students: *Writers write all they know about their topic, and then they look for what they don't know.*

George raises his hand to say, "How do we know what we don't know?"

Some of the kids giggle in agreement.

I can't help but smile, because I was expecting this. "That is exactly what I'm going to teach you today, George. Our strategy will help us think about what we know and then guide us to look for what we need to know. Are you ready?"

Students nod their heads in agreement. Their notebooks are already opened, their pens in hand. "Okay. Today, we're going to use our 'all about' strategy," I begin.

"Like 'all about' books we wrote in second grade?" asks Emma.

"I wrote some in first grade," Robert adds.

"Exactly. But in our notebooks, we're going to be quick about it.

You don't have to write in whole sentences—you can use phrases or words. Start with the topic you're writing about at the top—or your main idea," I pause while students do this. "Now we're going to do a fast write. You're going to write for two minutes, and, as fast as you can, jot down everything you know about your topic. Remember you don't have to explain it; you're just staking your claim on what you know about it."

Older students may need more time than just a couple of minutes, but two minutes of writing time is long for some third graders. It's not important that they finish the "all about" strategy during the mini-lesson. They can finish it during the workshop. Right now, I just want them to get the gist of the strategy.

"Okay, now I want you to take a moment to reread what you wrote." I pause as students reread. "Turn and talk to your partner and share something that surprised you about your list—maybe it was something on your list or something that you didn't put on your list. Maybe it's how much you know or that you thought you knew more."

I pause to give students time to talk with their partners. They start looking at one another's lists, and a couple of friends get in some debate about whether something is true or not.

"Ms. Buckner," George says. "Alexander wrote something on his list that is wrong, but he won't change it."

"That might happen, George. Sometimes we think we know something, but when we read more about the topic, we realize we misunderstood. Having a new stronger understanding is part of research. Let's not worry about that for now.

"What I do want you to do is reread your list again, but this time to yourself. Think about what isn't on the list—what don't you know or what aren't you sure is true? What are you wondering about? What do you want to know more about?"

Students are skimming their lists and looking up at me. "Go ahead and write some notes to yourself," I say. I show them a page in my notebook from when I did this for my duck story (see Figure 3.1). "Notice how I have check marks. Those are things I double-checked to make sure I was accurate."

"The question marks are for things you're really not sure about?" asks Camille, looking at my list.

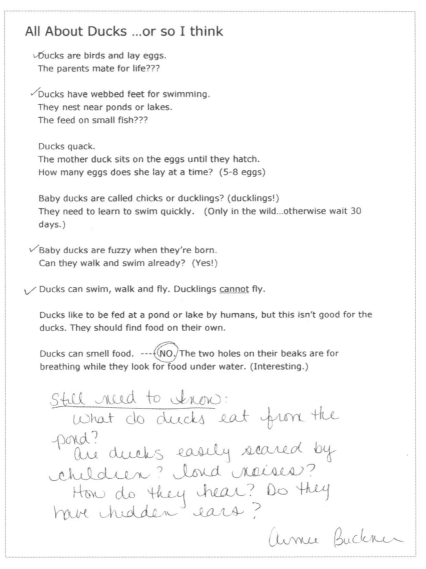

All About Ducks ...or so I think

Ducks are birds and lay eggs.
The parents mate for life???

Ducks have webbed feet for swimming.
They nest near ponds or lakes.
The feed on small fish???

Ducks quack.
The mother duck sits on the eggs until they hatch.
How many eggs does she lay at a time? (5-8 eggs)

Baby ducks are called chicks or ducklings? (ducklings!)
They need to learn to swim quickly. (Only in the wild...otherwise wait 30 days.)

Baby ducks are fuzzy when they're born.
Can they walk and swim already? (Yes!)

Ducks can swim, walk and fly. Ducklings <u>cannot</u> fly.

Ducks like to be fed at a pond or lake by humans, but this isn't good for the ducks. They should find food on their own.

Ducks can smell food. ---(NO.) The two holes on their beaks are for breathing while they look for food under water. (Interesting.)

Still need to know:
What do ducks eat from the pond?
Are ducks easily scared by children? loud noises?
How do they hear? Do they have hidden ears?

Annie Buckner

Figure 3.1 My "All About" List and Notes About Ducks

"Yes, or they're things I didn't know and added when I reread my list. It's okay to do this in your notebook, because your reader will *never know* you didn't know something."

Kids nod their heads and begin jotting in their notebooks. "Today, when you go off to write, think about the things you need to know to make your informational piece strong. These are the things you'll be paying attention to when you research, instead of the things you already know."

Kids are funny. They don't like to admit they don't know something, yet they seem relieved when they learn they don't have to research what they already know is fact. Teachers don't need to panic about wrong information, because oftentimes, as students read and research their work, they figure out their misunderstandings anyway. It's the beauty of research.

Strategy: Better Questions

At one of my summer professional development sessions, I was sharing some of my work that later appeared in this book. Teachers are great about giving feedback and tweaking ideas. (Thanks!) Every time I shared the work with different groups of teachers in different parts of the country, a similar question came up: What if we have a form with the research questions already on them?

It's tempting to give kids a form. I get it. Otherwise they grab at interesting facts and details that don't necessarily help their piece. Or they get so much information they just start copying out of a book or from a website, because they have no idea how they're going to manage all of the information. And even worse, some kids miss the whole point that there should be a main idea with supporting details throughout their piece. They just list fact after fact after fact. The CCSS ELA-Literacy-Writing standards 2, 4, and 9 refer to the organization of information with a main idea and supporting work. So we do need to move students away from random fact collecting to systematic information gathering.

But, I do get it. It might be a good idea to have a form with predetermined questions for small groups. Maybe you can use it as a model for how to take notes. But if you give all of the kids the same form, you're going to get the exact same report twenty times—just with a different animal. It will be like reading twenty Magic Tree House books in a row. Nothing against Magic Tree House—they're great for kids while they need the support of having the same characters with the same story elements over and over. Teachers don't need this kind of reading support, and by fourth grade our students don't need the kind of writing support a form with questions provides.

But the real reason I avoid a set format of research questions is that it teaches kids how to do one kind of report for one teacher. It doesn't teach the students how to be better writers the next time. And there is a next time. The CCSS ELA-Literacy-Writing standard 7 refers to conducting short research projects. Projects. Plural. We need to help move kids away from one big research unit on a single topic to shorter projects—on various topics—that allow students to practice how to gather information, which is CCSS ELA-Literacy-Writing standard 8.

"Boys and girls," I begin, "today we're going to talk about how writers ask themselves questions they don't know the answers to." This gets the students' attention, because I often tell them that I'll help them with questions they don't know the answers to. It's amazing how many questions kids ask to which they already know the answers.

"You mean like we're not allowed to ask you what we do when we finish a book, because we know what to do, right?" asks Robert.

"Right. Writers have to be careful that they don't spend too much time researching information they already know. They do need to confirm the accuracy of the facts they know, but it's a mistake to spend too much time on confirming rather than learning something new. For example, if I decide to write about Ernest Shackleton, I don't need to know that he's the captain of the *Endurance* or that he saved his crew. I already know all that. I can easily confirm that information with any resource about the *Endurance*, and I'll use that knowledge in my piece. However, if I know it, I probably read it, so it's already been written. Yes?"

My students nod. I can see that I've lost them a bit on that last part, but I trudge on so I can clarify and get them off to their writing.

"What I need to know is, How experienced was Shackleton before this trip? Had he been a captain before or was this his first voyage? I'll want to know something about his training and maybe how the men viewed him before and after the trip. These are things I don't know."

Now the lights are flickering behind their big eyes. Some kids nod their heads, and I get a verbal ohhh or two.

"Today, I want you to take a few minutes to reread your 'all about' list and the notes you wrote beside it," I explain.

"Because writers reread," Emma mumbles.

"Yes, because we reread our work to launch our new thinking. Today you'll think about what you don't know and create some questions that will help you write a better piece. Take a few moments now to reread your list and jot down some questions you would like to research."

Students begin rereading, thinking and making notes in their note-books. I watch for students who may look confused or unsure of what to do so I can redirect them. I notice that students don't always have a nice neat list of questions. Sometimes kids are writing in the margins (Figure 3.2), and sometimes the questions travel down the middle of the page without room for answers (Figure 3.3). I don't worry about

Figure 3.2 Notice that in her notebook, Rebecca wrote her questions around her "all about" entry from the day before. Her questions are in the margins: *Are all sharks vishis (vicious)? Are whale sharks vishis? body leghth (length)? Are sharks the fastest preteders (predators) in the ocean?* These questions will guide Rebecca's research as she starts to figure out how different whale sharks are from other sharks.

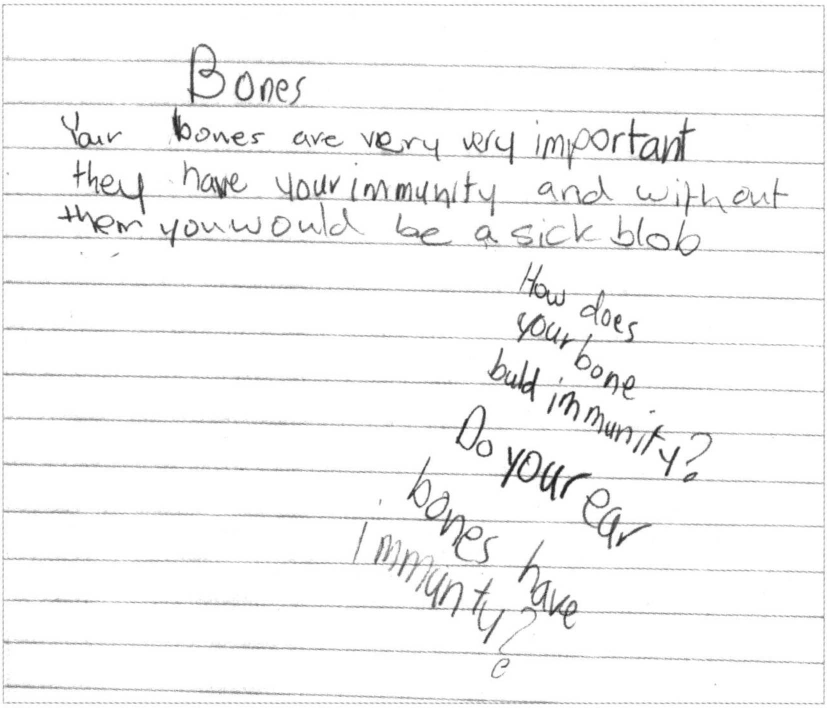

Bones

Your bones are very very important
they have your immunity and without
them you would be a sick blob

How does
your bone
buld immunity?
Do your ear
bones have
immunity?
e

Figure 3.3 Mahita, a fourth grader, wants to write about bones. First she writes a bit about what she knows about bones. She quickly focuses her work on the idea of immunity and then generates questions that might help her research.

that right now. This is a brainstorming session to help students realize there is more to know about the topic they've chosen.

Once most of the children have finished writing, I get their attention again. "I noticed all of you were able to think of at least one question to write down. Most of you had more. Turn to your partner, and partner A, share with partner B the questions you are going to try to answer in your research."

After the noise dwindles and kids wind up their conversations, I say, "Partner B, share with partner A the questions you are going to try to research today." Again the kids turn and talk. I see partners leaning into each other—both reading the same notebook. "Once you have the hang of this," I say, "you and your partner can find a place to begin researching and writing."

A hand goes up and a voice calls out, "What if we finish our questions?"

Camille replies, "You know the answer to that."

"I know, start finding out the answers," he says. And off they go to write.

Small-Group Support

It's tricky to help students figure out what they don't know. Some students will struggle with this. Here is a modified version of the same strategy that can be used with small groups.

Partner A, choose one of your "all about" topics from our writing yesterday. Reread what you wrote about it and summarize it for partner B. Partner B, while your partner is telling you about his or her topic, jot down on a sticky note any questions that pop into your head. When partner A is finished, partner B shares the questions and gives the sticky notes to partner A to put in his or her notebook. Partner A can then add on to the list, as this will help spark his or her thinking. Then repeat the process, switching roles.

Strategy: Take Note (Taking Notes with Text Closed After You Read)

Students read spread out around the room. Some are at computers, some are stretched out on large pillows on the floor, and still others read at their desks. I find a few kids writing—taking notes—from their book. I walk around to look over one child's shoulder. She's copying out of the book. I look across from her, where another child is writing notes—again copying.

"Girls, can you find a good stopping place so we can talk?" I interrupt them. Both of them finish what they are writing and look up.

"I noticed you are taking notes—how is that going?" I ask.

"Well, I found all these cool facts about the *Titanic,* and I'm writing them down," Rosa says.

"Me too," says Alana.

"When you write the facts down, whose words are you using?" I ask.

Both girls look at me with their brows furrowed in a confused way. "Are you copying the words from the book, or are you writing the fact in your own words?"

Both girls look down and say they were copying.

"I want you to try something," I begin. I take out some sticky notes and give some to each of the girls. "As you read, when you find a page that has something you want to remember, or you find an answer to one of your research questions, I want you to put the sticky note on the page and keep reading."

"What if we find three things on a page? Do we use three notes?" asks Alana.

"You could," I reply, "but you don't have to, because when you finish reading you can go back to the pages with sticky notes. When you go back, I want you to skim the page to remind yourself what you read. Then, take the sticky note out and close the book. Use the space on your note to jot down the information you wanted to remember."

"There isn't enough room on the sticky note," complains Rosa.

"There is enough room if you jot notes—phrases and key words that will help you remember the fact. You write enough to remember but not everything that is on the page."

"Like where it says in my book that you can tell the age of a horse from the color of its teeth. I don't write all of that. I'll write *teeth color=age,*" says Alana.

"You got it," I say. "This is going to help you paraphrase and take better notes."

"What if it's a fact, and I can't remember the number or how to spell a body part?" worries Rosa.

"Then you can go back and copy that out of the book, but don't copy all the words, because that's plagiarism," I reply.

The girls set off to read, stick, and note. The sticky notes they write will be placed in their notebooks on a page that has the title of the book or article they're reading. Then they'll have time to group their notes when they organize their writing. (See Figure 3.4.)

Sometimes students need a way not to copy every word. It's especially difficult for them to do if they are reading a text that is too difficult. In order to take notes, kids need to read easy or just-right books. It's easier for kids to paraphrase when they understand what they're reading.

Paraphrasing notes from a text is part of the process for recomposing, a strategy Steve Moline describes in his book *I See What You Mean* (2012). Students can also jot notes using sketches, diagrams, charts, time lines, or other ways they make up to restate what they learn from the text. I find it's helpful for kids to close the book or look away from the computer and then jot notes to lessen the temptation to copy outright. Students sometimes think this takes too long or is a waste of time; however, in the long run, it's time well spent.

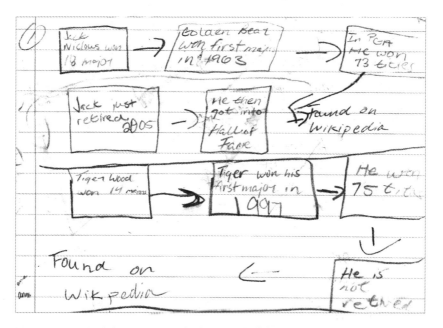

Figure 3.4 Jada did some research about one of the major golf tournaments held in Augusta, Georgia, known as the Masters Tournament. Instead of using sticky notes, she limited herself to small boxes she drew on a page. The arrows indicate the order in which she wrote the note.

Strategy: Sifting Through Text

"Hey, Ms. Buckner!" calls Anthony. "Did you know that every winter a septillion snowflakes fall? Septillion!"

"What's a septillion?" Zachary asks.

"It's a one with twenty-four zeroes after it," Anthony says. "A google is a one with a hundred zeroes after it."

"Anthony," I say, redirecting his attention to me. "That's a fascinating fact. How does it fit in with your writing work?" I ask.

"I'm studying tornadoes, but this was in the weather book I'm using," he said.

"Are you planning on writing it down in your notebook or just marveling for a few moments?" I ask.

"I'm marveling, Ms. Buckner," he says, giving me an odd look. "I'm only taking notes on tornadoes."

Not everyone understands the difference between facts we marvel over and facts we need to feed our informational pieces. Informational books for kids are filled with interesting fact bubbles and sidebars. Many times the fact is just that—interesting, but not related to the main idea. Unfortunately, some of my third and fourth graders want to collect only those facts. I'm not against these fascinating features, but I do want my students to determine whether or not information is relevant or important to their writing topic.

I attended the reading institute at Columbia University a couple of years ago. I love being in New York City, surrounded by people at the university who are eager to learn more about teaching reading. I get inspired by the instructors and by how smart they are. I'm awed by the research they've done and the conclusions they've drawn. Each time I go to one of their institutes, I learn how to take my teaching up a notch.

During the reading institute, my group leader showed us a diagram she called "boxes and bullets." It's a quick graphic that has a box large enough to fit a sentence in it and three bullets below it. Students read and they write the main idea in the box. Then they find three supporting details and jot those below the main idea.

My students use this as a guide for comprehending reading—especially as we tackle more difficult text.

It's also a great tool to help kids take notes and not copy out of books. It helps students determine importance, because they're constantly looking at the main idea in the big box. (See Figure 3.5.)

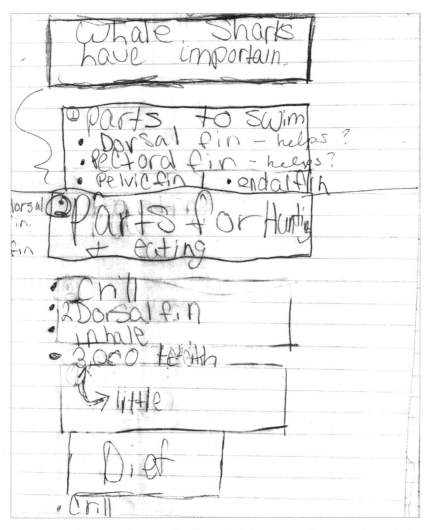

Figure 3.5 Rebecca uses boxes and bullets to help her organize her notes about whale-shark parts. Notice her main idea is at the top: Whale sharks have important [parts]. Then she has boxes below with bullets: parts to swim and parts for hunting and eating. The bullets list the facts or bits of information that she found in her research.

Boxes and bullets can be used in a lot of different ways, and the way they're used really depends on the length and complexity of the text. If a child is reading a one-page article on tornados, he or she probably needs only one set of boxes and bullets. If a student is reading an entire chapter with several subheadings, he or she may need a box and bullets organizer for each section. Once kids get the hang of this, they can draw their own sets of boxes and bullets in their notebooks.

We'll be able to use this kind of organizer again when students start to plan their pieces. It will help them envision their piece, find missing information, and develop a sense of what it means to outline.

Strategy: Words Their Way

I show the students two excerpts from my notebook.

> A:
> The boat was big and strong. It was going to go in cold water. This boat was like another boat and it wasn't supposed to sink. The other boat sank. It got stuck and fell into the sea. The people on the boat were scared but they lived.

> B:
> The Endurance was a strong ship. It was built to endure—withstand—even the ice-filled waters of Antarctica. Like the Titanic, though, this ship was not unsinkable. The ocean froze and the ice crushed the ship. Luckily, it took days for the ship to sink, so the crew disembarked safely. They survived, but they were stranded on a frozen ocean hundreds of miles from land.

"Which one of these paragraphs makes you think I did some research or that I know a lot about the *Endurance*?" I ask.

Rosa raises her hand first. "B is longer than A. There are more details," she says.

"There are more details," George chimes in.

"What do you mean, George?" I ask.

"Well, the first paragraph has just words like 'the boat' and stuff.

But the second one has the names of the boats and uses different words," he notices.

"You're both keen observers, Rosa and George," I say. "I do want to talk a little bit about what George said, though. One way a writer sounds really smart about their topic is by using specific nouns and verbs that belong to the topic. In our classroom, we might call these vocabulary words; in the writing world, we call these domain-specific words. These are the kinds of words you might find in a glossary, and they give the reader specific information about the subject."

I now pass out copies of a short excerpt from *National Geographic Explorer*, a classroom magazine my class receives.

Built for Survival

It sounds like the gecko had a tough night. To escape from two **predators**, *it soared through the air, lost its tail, and more. That is how many geckos survive in the world. How did one little lizard develop so many talents? Its abilities are the results of* **adaptations**. *When a* **species** *adapts, it changes over a long period of time. These changes can help an animal survive.* (Constantini 2010, 4)

Students glue the excerpt in their notebooks. Then they take a moment to read it. When I can see they've finished reading, I continue.

"Boys and girls, I'm going to read this to you. I want you to highlight or circle the words that tell you—the reader—that the writer knows his stuff. Ready?"

The children have done this kind of text mapping before, so they're ready to roll. I read the text to them and wait a few moments after I'm done so students can finish working.

"What kind of things did you notice?" I ask.

Alana starts, "It had bold print words—*predators, adaptations,* and *species.*"

"Those are interesting words, aren't they? Those are the kind of words an expert would use, don't you think?" I respond.

The children nod their heads.

"I noticed words like *escape, soared,* and *survive.* I felt like there was some action going on," Christopher adds.

"How interesting. Did anyone else notice some of these same words?" Most of the students' hands go up. "Do you know what you all did?" I ask with an exaggerated tone. "You found nouns and verbs, but not just any nouns and verbs. You found specific nouns that relate directly to the gecko and verbs that show action. Writers use these tools to keep their informational work interesting."

I open my notebook and signal to the children to do the same. "Today, as you continue to gather information for your piece, I want you to start a word list," I say. "You're going to keep track of interesting words you find in your research that you want to use later in your own writing. We're looking for something called *domain-specific* words."

On a chart titled *Writers use specific nouns and active verbs to keep their informational writing interesting*, I write the words *domain specific*.

"This means we're looking for words that an expert would use when talking about your topic."

"In other words," George interrupts, "vocabulary words."

"Yes, you could think of it that way," I say, as groans float up into the air like bubbles under water.

"You're keeping a list to help you remember to use them in your writing. If you already know the definition, you don't have to look it up. And if you don't know the definition, you can write a quick phrase or two to remind you of its meaning." (See Figure 3.6.)

The students are buying into it a bit more.

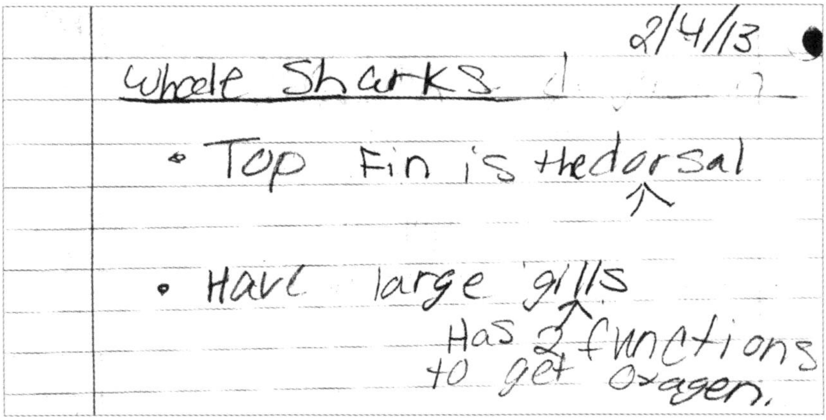

Figure 3.6 Rebecca starts a list of body parts at the bottom of a page in her notebook. It would be great for her also to have a diagram with these body parts labeled instead of just a list.

"The thing is, your word choice matters with every kind of writing. Not only will we craft our pieces to show our voice, but we also need to choose words that let our readers know we're smart about this subject."

Now I show them I want them to fold their next clean notebook page vertically in half. It makes a bit of a bookmark, and kids can find the page easily. This is where they'll keep the word list. If they don't want to fold a page, they can use a sticky note to mark the spot. It's important that kids can get to this page easily when they're researching and possibly taking notes on another page.

Strategy: Ask the Expert

Templeton the Rat might have been a writer if he weren't a rat. He saved everything; he was indeed a packrat. Writers aren't necessarily hoarders, like Templeton, but we save everything we might someday use in our writing. From snippets of conversations to things we observe and drama that unfolds in our lives: We save it.

Notebooks are great places to collect things. I've had students who have taped in leaves they found on the playground or tickets from a movie they saw over the weekend. I print out e-mails that are meaningful, trim them, and glue them into my notebook to reflect on later.

When students are researching a topic, there will come a time when they just need to ask somebody a question. Somebody who knows the answer. The information on the web isn't always sufficient or correct. Books and magazine articles only tell the reader so much, and a student doesn't have years to search and search for an answer.

For example, when I was working on my fictional story about ducks last year, I ran into a question that I knew wouldn't be answered in any book or website. My story is about ducks trapped in a schoolyard, and they need to get to the pond. The only solution is to lead the ducks through the school. Originally, I had planned to have the students at the school leave a trail of breadcrumbs for the mama duck and ducklings to follow. Since I wanted the story to be realistic, I contacted the Georgia Wildlife Resources Division and spoke with a ranger with extensive duck experience. I simply asked, "Could I get ducks to follow a trail of breadcrumbs through a school?" He told me I could, but that it would not be something they would encourage. He gave me some other ideas of how to lure the ducks—for example, with a duck call. He told me it's important not to feed wild animals so that they will continue to find food on their own. All of this made a difference to my story, even though it was a fiction piece. The same process can help a writer with an informational piece.

With the technology available to us in schools, there is no reason kids can't contact an expert in the field. They can e-mail someone, leave a comment on a blog, make a phone call, or even do a face-to-face interview via the Internet. Of course, they could also see the person in human form.

Students can also talk with other students who know a lot about a subject. Towner, the student with pet chickens, knew a lot more about raising chickens than our science teacher did. So when it was time to incubate and hatch chicks, our science teacher naturally sought out his help. That's what people do; they go to experts to ask for help.

When students will go the route of talking with an expert, I have them set aside a page in their notebooks with the person's name and contact information. This way they'll have it in a safe place.

On this page, students spend about five minutes generating the questions they have for the experts. I also ask them to note where they have already looked for the information—did they check a website or consult a magazine?

Once they're ready, they contact the person and note on the page how and when they made contact. Did they call? Send an e-mail? Post on a blog? It's possible they won't be able to contact the expert that day. That's why it's important to document the process in the notebook. Once the experts return the students' calls or e-mail back, the students can refer to that page to jot their thinking down. (It's always a good idea to send a thank-you note if someone takes a lot of time to help a student.)

Strategy: Ready, Set, Action!

I love watching students play on the playground. One year, my fourth graders were passing around books from the Warriors series. They had formed an after-school Warriors book club, and now they were playing Warriors on the playground. Each of the kids involved was a cat from one of the clans featured in the series. They designated different areas of the playground as "dens." And from there, they reenacted different scenes from the books. How cute is that?

As a parent, I love observing my kids when they're around their peers. I listen to their conversations as I drive them to and from the basketball game. I watch them interact with kids they don't know at the roller rink. And I pay attention to the things they choose to do alone. Observing them in action has kept me informed.

Writers do the same thing. They observe their subjects when they can. My friend and author Lola Schaefer is working on a manuscript about a girl who lives near a dolphin sanctuary. Lola went to Key West to observe dolphins and talk to experts about some of the situations she was planning for her story. It would be very difficult for Lola to write a chapter book about dolphins if she had never observed one.

Students can't observe their subjects every time they write. For example, it would be impossible to observe the Battle of Gettysburg, but there are plenty of reenactments and simulations on the computer that they could watch. Finding ways for students to observe their subjects will make their writing more believable.

"Boys and girls, today we're going to talk about how writers observe," I begin. "When writers work on informational pieces, they often try to go to the places they're writing about or see the animals that will be in their stories. It's important to get a sense of the real thing."

"What if you can't go? I mean, we're just kids," says Emma.

"Well, we have plenty of technology that will let you take virtual trips to the places you need to observe. We also have ways you can observe animals and people you may be studying."

"What if my person is dead?" asks George.

"Depending on the person, their house may be preserved and have a website. Or, there may be old films or pictures of the person. The idea isn't to find ways not to observe your topic; the idea is to be creative in order to observe," I counter.

"You can keep your observations on your subject in your notebook," I continue. "You can write in full sentences and paragraphs, or you can jot phrases. It's up to you."

Observing a topic in action is easier today than ever. The CCSS support the guided use of technology and digital sources to research and produce writing pieces. Think about all of the resources we can set up for our students or guide them toward: streaming educational videos; websites with live webcams and/or video clips; museum sites or official web pages; or appropriate videos on YouTube. Observing a person or place to gather information may be new to students, and it can be a bit of a challenge. However, these observations will provide key details as they draft their pieces and try to show, not tell.

Strategy: Stick It or Flick It

We've been gathering information for our pieces for a few days. Books are stacked on desks and chairs throughout the classroom. There are rainbows of sticky notes slipping out of each book, holding places where students have found information they plan to use. Inside their notebooks, the sticky notes are plentiful too. And if I look closely enough, I'm bound to find a note sticking to the bottom of someone's shoe or on the sleeve of a sweater.

There is a brief moment when I start to panic—*too many sticky notes*. Then I take a deep breath and get ready to teach my students to stick it or flick it.

"Boys and girls, today we're going to address all of these sticky notes you have been gathering. To start off, I want you to go back in your notebook where you wrote about the main idea of your piece. Please reread that to refresh your memory."

I wait a moment while students find their places and read, then I go on. "Now I want you to flip to the page where you wrote down your big questions about the topic. The questions that you didn't know the answers to before you started researching." Again, I wait as the students flip through their notebooks, find the page, and skim their questions.

"Today you are going to go through all the sticky notes you've gathered. Look at the information you jotted or sketched on each one. Decide if it supports your main idea or helps to answer one of your questions."

"What if they don't?" asks Camille.

"If they don't, then put them to the side. We'll deal with those later."

I give the students time to work with their partners, sorting through their sticky notes and determining which are needed and which are not. As students finish, I gather them back to the whole group.

"What did you discover about your sticky notes?" I ask.

Robert raises his hand. "George and I had a lot of notes that didn't match our main idea. They were cool facts, but they don't go with our piece."

"That's a bummer, Robert. It happens to writers all the time. We find out this fascinating bit of information and we save it. Then we realize, after a while, we don't really need it."

"We found sticky notes that had just one word on them, and I couldn't remember what they were about," says Camille.

I laugh. "That happens to me too. Did anyone find sticky notes that helped to answer your questions or supported your main idea?" I ask hopefully.

Students raise their hands. Inside, I gave a big sigh of relief. "Okay, we're going to keep those. You can reorganize your notes to keep the ones that answer the same question on one page. Then stick the notes that answer a different question on another page, and so on," I explain.

"What about these we don't need?" asks Robert as he gazes down at a pile of discarded notes.

"If you're finished with them, rip off the sticky part to throw away and recycle the bottom half."

The students continue sorting, sticking, and recycling their notes. Once this is finished, they'll be ready to begin their draft.

* * *

Not every student will need every strategy discussed in this chapter each time he or she writes. It's important to know your students' needs and select strategies accordingly. Just as when we teach personal narrative, we build on strategies with each informational piece kids write. The CCSS specify that students should write more than one informational piece a year. This leaves teachers with opportunities to teach students different ways to gather information and keep it organized. Eventually, students will have enough strategies in their toolbox from which to choose when they need to do some research.

CHAPTER 4

Predrafting Strategies

Playing a sport is a lot like writing. You practice and practice and practice. You research what to do to get better and follow the tips of a mentor. Then you are ready for the big game, and you have a pregame pep talk with your coach. You plan your strategy of attack and envision how you want the game to go. While playing the game, you may need to improvise and change your original thinking to compete against the other team. In the end, there is a score and a postgame meeting to make changes for the next round of practices and/or game.

Just like in sports, writers practice, research, and follow a mentor. They have a pregame strategy, too. Before drafting, they often take some time to envision how the piece will go. They think about the form, organization, and outcome of the piece. Writers prepare for their draft and then revise—sometimes as they go and sometimes after the draft is finished—to make the piece their best work. They reflect on their work and make changes and set goals for the writing yet to come.

When students are preparing to write an informational piece, they often just want to jump in and write it without a predraft strategy. They don't want to think about the organization, focus, or vision for the final piece. Yet, prewriting serves a purpose. If our students can take the time to use one or two predrafting strategies, their drafts may be more organized and more in line with what they want to do for a final piece. This sets the student up for fewer necessary revisions. I'm not saying that just by using predrafting strategies the draft will be perfect and won't need revisions. Just like athletes in sports, writers are always adjusting to make their piece better. However, with some foresight and preparation, young writers can avoid some drastic revisions.

Like most people, I have bad habits. I have to fight to keep them in check, with better results on some days than others. As a writing teacher, I sometimes get caught up in the calendar frenzy—feeling like I'm running out of time to get everything finished. When that happens, I've caught myself wanting to cut the notebook work down and get the students writing a rough draft quickly so we can move on to revision. In my lesson plans, this looks like a good way to move through the whole writing process, but in reality, moving too quickly makes a lot more work for my young writers.

Writers of all ages need to plan, talk, rearrange, plan again, and talk some more before they actually write. We do this in different ways. Last night, a friend called me to talk through some ideas she wanted to use in a letter to her daughter. In a second-grade classroom that I recently visited, students took time to talk with their writing partners plus another set of partners to tell and retell their story before drafting. Don Graves referred to this as rehearsal (Murray 1978), and we see it a lot in the lower elementary grades. Yet, in the upper elementary grades, it's just as important for students to have that chance to talk through their drafts—making changes as they go along—before they actually write. In doing so, students have already made some revisions—quite painlessly—and are more likely to have a stronger first draft.

Thinking about how writers organize their work to write an informational piece and how readers need certain transition cues from the writer, I started using some predrafting strategies to help my students write a better first draft.

Strategy: Topic Change-Up

I use the "topic change-up" strategy when most of my students have finally decided on what their topic will be for their informational piece. We're at a point where the students need to start making decisions about how they'll write their piece. Will they write a feature article or a short essay? Will they write a travel guide or a picture book? Will they compare and contrast their topic with something else, or will they ask their readers true/false questions? Finding the energy in a topic is—in part—finding the right way to write it. (See Figure 4.1.)

Figure 4.1 Possible Formats for "Topic Change-Up"

These are the formats I chose to use with students. Teachers should choose five formats with which their students are familiar.

Newspaper article
Advice column
Annotated top-ten list
Picture book: narrative
Picture book: informational
Graphics only: diagram, table, map, chart, illustration with caption
Feature article for a magazine
Informational poem
Reader's theater
Time line

"Okay writers," I begin, "you're in for a treat. Most of you have decided on a big topic for your informational piece. Many of you have the main idea for your piece as well. Now we're going to see what kind of writing will be best for your idea."

The students wiggle a bit, indicating they are somewhat unsure of what's about to happen. "What you're going to do is write about your topic. I am going to say a kind of writing or an organizational style that I want you to use (see Figure 4.2). The tricky part is I'm going to keep changing my mind. I don't want you to stop writing or start over. Just keep writing."

Figure 4.2 Possible Organizational Styles for "Topic Change-Up"

Try the same strategy with different forms of organization. Choose two or three of these organizational patterns:

Chronological (a day in the life, life cycle, year by year)
Step-by-step, how-to, or process
Question/answer or True/False
Problem/solution
Order of importance
Compare/contrast

George's brows are scrunched as he raises his hand. "I'm not sure I get it." His comment is greeted with several sighs of relief from other students who are a bit confused.

"I will start by asking you to write as if you were writing a feature article," I explain. "Then, after a few minutes, I may say 'poem,' and you'll continue writing, but you'll make that part like a poem. Then I may say 'Who Would Win?' book, and you'll continue writing, but this time you'll compare your topic to something else."

George is nodding his head. "Okay," he says.

And we're off.

I wait until the second or third informational writing study before I use this strategy. Students need to have a handle on several ways to write informational text before trying this. However, it's a great way to help students clarify how they want to write a piece. (It's also a great assessment tool.) Sometimes kids are convinced that they want to write a picture book when in reality their topic would make a better magazine article.

Strategy: Digging Deep

There is power in just one word. Power to lead our thinking in several different directions. Many times, one word describes a loved one or an enemy, a theme of a book or a movie review. One word is sometimes better than a thousand of them.

When my students are struggling to find meaning with their topics— something more than *I like snakes so I'll write about snakes*—I tell them it's time to dig deep. But how can they do that? It just takes one word.

I gather a small group of students who are having trouble finding their main idea for the informational piece they need to write. They're stuck on wanting to just write a report and tell all about their topic. In order to lift the level of their writing, I need to help them find a piece of the topic that holds meaning for them.

"What word do you think of when you think about your topic?" I begin. "When you think about dogs or football, what one word comes to mind?"

Robert says, "My topic is football, so my word would be *tough*."
Michelle says, "My topic is rabbits. My word is *cuddly*."

Slowly we work our way around the group as they connect their topic to one word. "Now, write your word at the top of a clean page in your notebook. I'm going to time you for three minutes. I want you to write the entire time, even if you wander from your topic. Write about your word and what it means in relation to your topic. So Robert will begin writing about why football is tough, and Michelle will begin writing about bunnies being cuddly." I start the timer, and the students begin working.

Usually, students get off to a strong start and begin to waver once their initial and obvious connections are over. It's important for me to keep encouraging them to dig deep—to keep thinking of this word in relation to the topic. If needed, I give the kids a couple more minutes. I want them to get about a page in their notebook.

Robert's entry:

Tough. Football is tough. It's hot and there are a lot of things you have to wear. People keep trying to tackle you. It's also tough because the coaches aren't nice like your teachers. They're nice but they yell. It's sometimes hard to be yelled at and then keep playing. It's also tough because there are a lot of kids on the field and sometimes I don't know where the ball has gone. Then I'll look around and the other team has it in the end zone. Tough luck.

Michelle's entry:

Bunnies are soooo cuddly. Well I've never held a rabbit before. They look cuddly. They look soft and fuzzy, like a stuffed animal. I wonder if a rabbit would bite you if you tried to cuddle it. I'd have to catch one first. They hop fast and they don't like to be by people. Sometimes I see one hopping through my back yard. I want to go grab it, but it might bite me. My mom tells me not to play with wild animals. I think she's afraid the animal will bite me.

As the students finish, I give them one more nudge before sending them off to write on their own. "When you go to write more today, I want you to reread your work. If you have more to say, keep writing. If you find a sentence that brings your writing in a different direction, then use a different page and begin writing about that."

Strategy: Box It Up

I met Ethan in Mrs. Bean's second-grade classroom in Forsyth County, Georgia. His writer's notebook is filled with illustrations and words. He's an artist, and he sees his stories in pictures. When writing his personal stories or fiction stories, he often draws out the story first and then he adds the words. This is a great strategy for young writers moving from pictorial representation of words to using letters to represent sounds and eventually full words. But Mrs. Bean and I want to make sure Ethan is able to convey his meaning with mostly words in addition to conveying his meaning visually.

Ethan is a visual learner. He finds visual text a more accessible means of communication than words alone. In his book *I See What You Mean: Visual Literacy K–8,* Steve Moline (2012) helped me understand the value of students' work when using visual cues instead of just words. Because I don't think in terms of pictures and spaces, I sometimes forget that visual literacy is a form of communication that is useful to many writers of informational texts.

I move to confer with Ethan by squatting down next to him and taking a moment to observe what he is doing. The class is working on informational writing. Ethan has chosen to write a "Who Would Win?" book—comparing king cobra snakes to a two-headed snake he had read about.

Ethan has folded his notebook page in half vertically. On each half, he is drawing boxes to mirror each other. One column (or half of the sheet) is for two-headed snakes and the other half is for king cobra snakes. In each box, Ethan has a sketch with some words (see Figure 4.3).

"Ethan, can I talk with you for a few minutes?" I begin.

"Sure," he says without looking up. I wait for him to finish the box he's drawing. He puts his pencil down and looks at me.

Figure 4.3 Ethan's Two-Column Notebook Page Comparing Two-Headed Snakes to King Cobras

"Will you tell me about how you're working on your writing today?" I ask.

Ethan immediately starts to flip to previous pages to show me what he's been working on—how his book is going to be about king cobras versus two-headed snakes.

"That's fascinating, Ethan. I didn't know there were many two-headed snakes."

"There aren't, but they're really cool!" he says.

"So tell me what you're doing on this page," I say as I turn back to the page with boxes laid out.

"Oh. I'm just putting my thinking down. The words help you read the picture."

"This is brilliant," I say. And I mean it. Part of me worries that Ethan is stuck in the pictorial writing stage, but, knowing his work, I know he is more than capable of writing more words than using pictures. The other part of me realizes that Ethan is a visual learner and that pictures are important to his work. So much so that he's being careful to choose words that will clarify his pictures to the reader.

"Ethan, why did you choose pictures for these facts rather than words alone?" I ask.

Ethan thinks a moment and then responds, "I think the pictures are more interesting. Plus, I can get my point across with a picture of the two-headed snake and the word *unusual*. I don't have to write all the words *two-headed snakes are unusual. Most snakes have one head.* I'd rather draw the picture."

I do want to encourage Ethan to develop his piece with more writing. But, for the purpose of the prewriting, these boxes and phrases are doing the trick to help him think about comparing and contrasting the two kinds of snakes. Later, as he moves toward his draft, I can nudge him to look at Jerry Pallotta's Who Would Win? books to demonstrate how Pallotta writes a paragraph *and* uses pictures on each page. (As a teacher, it's hard not to want to help students lengthen their writing when it can be longer. Yet, at the same time, I need to respect the use of graphics and their importance with informational writing.)

During the share time, I put Ethan's work under an ELMO camera to display it on the screen. "When I sat down next to Ethan," I say to the class, "he was working on drawing boxes. *Drawing* boxes during *writing* time." I emphasize the words *drawing* and *writing* with mock irritation.

"I asked Ethan, what was he doing with these boxes and how was it going to help his writing? And writers, I'll be honest, I thought Ethan was avoiding writing today. I thought he just wanted to draw pictures. I thought he was wasting writing time. But . . . I . . . was . . . *wrong*!" (Big gasp from the crowd.)

"Ethan told me that he was using the boxes and pictures to help readers understand some of his big ideas as he compared and contrasted these snakes. You see, he knows pictures and illustrations are going to be important to his work. He knows that the words and pictures need to work together, and sometimes the best way to get a reader to pay attention to a picture is to put just a few words in the caption or label. Ethan knows he wants to have the words and pictures next to each other. So instead of writing, writing, writing and then trying to squeeze in a picture or two *if* they fit, he is planning, planning, planning for his pictures and words to work together."

Stunned silence.

"What I want you to know is that if it is helpful to you to use pictures with some words to relate some facts to your readers, it's a good idea. That counts as writing, because not only are you communicating important information with your reader, but also you're envisioning the layout of your book. If you think Ethan's strategy of using picture boxes and short word phrases will help you keep track of facts, then you should do this in your notebook. If you're on a roll, though, you can tuck this idea in the back of your mind and use it another time."

The children go back to work. Some start sketching boxes to try out Ethan's strategy. Others just keep writing.

As a teacher of writing, it's important to realize that not all writers write the same way. Our mini-lessons at the beginning of the workshop are short for a reason. The nitty-gritty teaching and learning happen during the conferences. I teach my mini-lesson to all of my students the same way at the same time. Conferences allow me to teach each student differently as needed. In the upper elementary grades, we often hold off on page layout until the draft is finished. Yet, Ethan showed me that, like anything in the writing process, there are valid reasons for doing things differently.

Strategy: Which Way Do I Go?

My students are itching to write the first drafts of their informational pieces. Before they set off to write, I gather them for a quick strategy lesson. I remind the students to bring their notebooks, pens, and several sticky notes each.

"Boys and girls, I know many of you are ready to draft," I begin. Heads nod, and I continue, "Sometimes writers start drafting without giving much thought to how they're going to organize their piece. This might work out okay with poems and narratives, but it's harder to do this well when writing informational pieces.

"Today, I'm going to ask you to plan your piece. On each sticky note—and you can get more if you need them—I want you to write the big idea for each section of your piece. Take a moment to do that now."

I pause and watch the children write on their notes. Some students get up to grab some larger stacks of sticky notes and then pass them around to others. Once most of the students are finished, I continue.

"When I go to write a book, I have to talk to my editor about what I think will come first, second, and third. When I write, sometimes I change my mind. That's okay, because I just e-mail my editor and say I rearranged some topics. But I have a plan or an outline to start with.

"Talk to your writing partner about your plan for how your informational piece will go. Put your sticky notes in that order across two clean pages in your notebook."

I show them with my notebook how this might look. Then I give them time to turn and talk with their partners. This only takes a few minutes. The kids usually have a good idea of their sections and their order in the piece. Using the sticky notes is a tactile way for them to confirm their thinking and to hold their thinking over several days.

"Good job, everyone. Now, when you go to draft your informational piece, you can follow your notes. Write about one topic at a time. If, as you write, you decide that you need to reorder your notes, that's okay. The sticky notes will stick again in a different order. Once you're finished writing about a topic on your note, put a check on it so you remember which section you're writing next."

This is an easy, movable outline, essentially. It helps kids think about how they'll organize their work—which subtopic will go first, second, and last. But the real beauty of it, for me, is that it's not written in ink on a page. It's adaptable to the writer changing his or her mind.

The following graphic represents Haley's sticky notes for her informational piece about polar bears. The first set of notes is her initial plan for writing. The second set of notes reflects how she rearranged the information after rehearsing the order with her partner.

Set 1:

I use sticky notes because I like kids to be able to move the notes around as they rehearse. However, there are a variety of graphic organizers and visual texts that can also serve this purpose. For example, if a student is writing a how-to piece, he or she might want to use a flowchart. If a student is comparing and contrasting, he or she may want to use a Venn diagram or a table to plan before writing. This kind of work is what Steve Moline (2012) refers to as visual thinking. It allows students to quickly see the big information and to organize it before drafting their piece.

Strategy: Talking to Myself

The problem with hands-free cell phones is that I can no longer tell who is talking to themselves in the car. As a kid, it used to crack me up when we were stopped next to someone talking in the car only to notice they were alone. To be honest, I talk to myself all the time. I practice how a parent conference might go or how I'm going to approach a touchy subject with my teenager. I talk to myself to practice new presentations or even just to fill the quietness of the house when my kids are away. (Okay, my kids are always home, but they'll leave some day, and I'll talk to myself then too.)

Writers talk through their stories before, during, and after they write them. We think about the stories in our heads and replay scenes over and over until we think we'll write it right. We call colleagues and editors to talk over ideas we have—all in the name of preparing to write. Basically, we're rehearsing.

My students are getting to the age when they can write longer stories and informational pieces. We don't always have time for them to talk with three different people to rehearse their work before they write. Yet, it makes writing so much easier if kids have a chance to rehearse before committing their ideas to paper.

My students are now in the habit of finding at least two people with whom they can rehearse their piece. For the third rehearsal, I encourage students to write in their notebooks—talking themselves through their plan. Sometimes kids will jot a list as they think through the piece. Other times they'll write a quick paragraph or two. And still others will draw a sketch, map, or chart to get out their thinking. But it's a way to get their juices flowing and make any more changes to the organization and subtopics they're using before writing it all down.

Here is an example from Haley's notebook (grade 3):

Topic: Summer Camp
Rehearsal—
I want to write like I'm taking people on a tour of the camp. I'll start with the camp entrance and then take them to the cabins. After the cabins, I'll write about going to the lake and the hiking activities. We'll end up at a campfire. I think I'll tell stories along the way.
entrance—setting what the camp looks like
cabins—meeting new friends and having to sleep on a top bunk
the lake—tell about the swimming and canoeing activities

hiking—describe the woods and what you see on the hikes

campfire—tell readers about the fun we have around the
campfire at the end of each day

Haley's jot list would also do well on a map of the camp with little notes in each place. Haley chose the list, but she could have done it differently.

Here is an example from Robert's notebook (grade 3):

My article is about how football is a tough sport. I'm going to start with a quick story of when I was playing football and got hurt. My first section will be about all of the safety equipment players wear. It must be a tough sport if you have to wear so much stuff. Then my second section will focus on tackling. Tackling is not easy, especially with all the pads you wear. There is a right way to do it and a wrong way. Plus, it hurts to be tackled, sometimes. My third section will be how it is tough to catch a fast runner. I'm learning how to be a faster runner so I can catch up and tackle someone. I'm going to end with how my mom always comments on how many bruises I have during football season and how the weather can make playing even tougher.

Robert chose to write in paragraph form. If he wanted a more visual representation, he could have made a flowchart indicating his topics and using arrows to demonstrate what would come first, second, and third.

Lifting the Level for Students Who Are Ready

After reading entries from predrafting strategies in the students' notebooks, I can see that the writers have a solid sense of what they'll write and the order in which they'll do it. Some students will get the hang of organizing their thoughts more quickly and may not need as many predrafting strategies. In this case, students may move right to an outline. To practice writing a formal outline for an informational piece, students can adapt the informal outline from their notebook entry.

For example, based on Robert's preceding entry, an outline might look like this:

I.   Introduction
    A. Story about getting hurt
II. Equipment for safety
    A. Helmets
    B. Pads
    C. Mouth guards
    D. Cleats
III. Tackling
    A. How to do it correctly
    B. Tackling a player on the run
IV. Weather
    A. How hot weather affects players
    B. How cold weather affects players
    C. How rainy weather affects players
V.   Conclusion

Although this outline is not fully developed, it is the outline of what Robert rehearsed in his notebook. It's a good transition for him to see the information he plans to write about in an organized way. Many elementary students have trouble going directly to the outline without the middle step of rehearsing what they plan to write. As they get better at rehearsing their writing verbally and in a quick notebook entry, they'll be able to see the outline as a more sophisticated way to rehearse and organize their work.

Drafts

I love author visits. I hear repeatedly from authors that they are often surprised by what they write, that sometimes, they start to write and the story takes a turn they hadn't expected. This doesn't mean that the author just started writing one day and out popped this great story. It doesn't mean that the author started writing a mystery and it turned into a poem. Professional writers do a lot of work before they start drafting. This allows them to think about a lot of different possibilities and to have a plan to start with for the draft. Then as they write, if they want to "revise as they go" and take a turn in their writing, a professional writer can.

I try to explain this to my students. The prep work we do in our notebooks—the prewriting, the research, and the predrafting—is important thinking that writers do. It's not necessary that every student use every strategy described in this chapter every time they prepare to write a draft. As I reread this chapter, I think about how many (not all) of these strategies I have used in small groups, based on what my students have needed. Robert and Michelle were very factual writers; they needed to dig a little deeper to feel something for their topic. George is the kind of kid who doesn't always consider different possibilities for his writing, so the "topic change-up" was good for him.

Writers are all different, and we need to be aware of how our students approach their writing. Knowing this will help us determine which strategies are best for a mini-lesson, which strategies are best for a small group or even a conference, and which strategies are not needed this time around. The important thing to remember is not to burden your students with so many predrafting strategies that they lose the energy to write their draft. The pregame strategy meeting is brief and often inspiring as athletes envision their win on the field. The same should go for our writers. Keep it brief, but substantive enough for students to have a vision and a plan for their writing. Goooo, writers!

CHAPTER 5

Strategies to Craft
Informational Pieces

My two sixth graders came home from school one day last spring with a writing assignment in social studies. The assignment came with a list of questions the kids had to answer about an animal they chose. So basically, everyone would have the same report but with a different animal.

I asked, "What kind of writing support is your teacher giving you?"

"What?" my son, Michael, asked.

"What kind of help is he giving you? Is he teaching you how to research or take notes?" I asked.

"No," Michael said.

"Is he teaching you how to blend narrative into your informational work?" I asked.

"No, Mom! We can do this ourselves. It's an out-of-school assignment," my son said defensively.

"Aimee, this isn't writing class," added my stepdaughter, Syd. "It's social studies. We're doing animals in Australia," she told me, as if that would explain it all.

I realized I needed to be more parent than teacher for my kids. Stepping back, I watched them research their animals, take notes, and create their writing pieces. Both of them dutifully answered the questions on their note page, as assigned. Not a bit more information was added. Then my son wrote a typical report-style piece—very informative, with five paragraphs. Wikipedia couldn't have done it better. My stepdaughter wrote her piece from the point of view of the animal. She was thrilled when her social studies teacher told her that in all the years he's given this assignment, this was the first time anyone had written from the animal's point of view.

"Syd, where did you get the idea to write from the animal's point of view?" I asked.

"I saw that book on your desk," she replied. "I read it and thought I could do that."

"What book?" I asked.

"The groundhog one," she said and left the room to grab it. She brought back *Groundhog Gets a Say* by Pamela Curtis Swallow (2005). It's written as if the groundhog is being interviewed. He tells the reporter all there is to know about groundhogs and then some.

I should note that my kids do not see me as an expert on anything. I've learned to be mom at home and to support their teachers the best I can. But I can't help noticing how even without help, mentor texts shaped the different styles of writing for my kids. Michael, who wrote off his notes page, wrote a five-paragraph essay on his animal that would make any English teacher proud. Sydney, who happened to read a different kind of book, wrote an imaginative yet informative piece about her animal. The common thread is that they both relied on mentor texts—emulating what they saw other writers do.

In the classroom, we can support learning from mentor texts by having mentor texts available for students to look at during their writing process. We can use the texts for mini-lessons, so that we can highlight certain passages and give explicit instruction about how writers approach various kinds of writing. By planning strategically, based on what our students need to know and what they're ready to learn, mentor texts can be a powerful tool in the hands of both teachers and the students.

Luckily, mentor texts do not have to be on the exact same topics as the topics on which students are writing. We can teach students to learn about the writing in mentor texts at their reading level, even if the books are not on the exact topics they're writing about that day.

Sydney was writing about manatees, and her mentor text was about a groundhog. All too often, we rely only on the same kind of texts and topics as those our students write. This isn't wrong, and it is helpful in a lot of different ways. Writers do ask, How have other people written about dogs? Or, How have other people written a biography? But writers also think, *I like the way Pamela Swallow wrote*

Groundhog Gets a Say. *I wonder if I can do that with my topic.* We can help our students become better writers by stretching their thinking and having them ask, *How do other writers do this kind of writing?* In this way, we open up the possibilities for our students.

Strategy: Creating Images

I love San Francisco. It's a great city—not too big and not too small. It has a great art museum, the Legion of Honor, which houses one of the largest privately owned collections of Rodin sculptures. It was here I first saw *The Kiss,* and I fell in love. As I stood in front of the sculpture, I was taken by how real it seemed. Romance emanates from the statue, bringing warmth to the otherwise cold stone. I thought about how Rodin must have created this piece. It started as a large chunk, and with vision and precision, he chipped away at it, bit by bit. I imagine he had a general idea of what he wanted to create. But Rodin had to focus on every detail to get it just the way he wanted it. Eventually this masterpiece was finished. Amazing.

As writers, we need to envision the possibilities for our writing pieces. Sometimes we can picture the piece as a whole, but at other times, we need to focus on just chipping away at a part of it. I don't mean taking things out but rather fine-tuning the details—creating the images that will hold our readers' attention and even their hearts.

In my classroom, my students are often trying to put so many facts into their pieces that they forget to create images for their readers. Even with informational writing, it's important to remember how readers comprehend text. Readers need to be able to visualize, and as writers, it's our job to create images for them.

"Writers, today we're going to talk about helping your readers visualize the information in your work," I begin. My students are gathered around me—some are sitting with their legs crossed, others are on beanbags or pillows, and a few are sitting in chairs they've pulled up from their desks. They all have their notebooks.

I continue, "Sometimes when I write an informational piece, I forget to help my reader picture my ideas in his or her head. Even worse,

when I'm reading an informational piece, it's harder for me to understand the text when I can't picture what's going on in my head. Writers
give clues or images for their readers to think about as they read."

Emma raises her hand. "I thought that's what the pictures are for
in nonfiction books."

"That's a good point, Emma. But, how many of you have ever read
a magazine article or an informational book and have . . . skipped . . .
the pictures?" I ask, emphasizing the word *skipped*. Slowly a few hands
go up. "Come on, admit it. How many of you skip the pictures and just
read?" I ask again as I raise my own hand. In truth, I sometimes do skip
pictures and captions unless I think I need them.

"I never skip the pictures," says George. "They're the best part."

"True, pictures can be interesting and give us important information. I think as we get used to chapter books not having pictures, we
sometimes forget to really look at them in nonfiction texts.

"So, writers need to be prepared for the readers to skip the pictures. Readers won't skip the words, though. As writers, we're going to
focus on images for our readers."

I pass out copies of a typed (and trimmed, ready to be glued into
their notebooks) excerpt from *The Tarantula Scientist* by Sy Montgomery (2004).

> *Even for a big mammal like a human, the sight of a Goliath birdeater
> tarantula rushing out of her burrow takes your breath away. She's
> not even full grown, but her head is the size of a fifty-cent piece. Her
> abdomen is bigger than a quarter. All of her body, including each of
> the seven segments of her eight strong, long legs, is covered with rich,
> deep reddish brown hairs, some of them half an inch long.* (8)

I give the students time to glue the excerpt onto the next clean page
of their notebooks. As we're waiting, some of the children begin reading the piece. I see two boys making circles with their fingers, trying to
visualize just how big this spider is—this not fully grown spider.

When the students are mostly ready, I begin reading the excerpt. I
read it a second time and ask the students to mark—circle, underline,
highlight—any phrases that help them visualize this Goliath spider.

After they've talked with a partner about what they marked and how that helped them visualize, we regroup and discuss what the writer did to help the reader.

"What did you notice?" I ask.

Cameron raises his hand. "I liked how he used money to show us how big the spider is. A quarter doesn't sound big, but when you look at a quarter and think, that's the size of its abdo—ab—abdomen, that's a pretty big spider!"

"I saw some of you trying to make circles with your fingers to 'see' its size. You're right though, Cameron, sometimes writers use comparisons to things readers use every day—like coins—to help us make a picture in our mind."

"I liked the phrase 'eight strong, long legs,'" says Sally. "It kind of rhymes and it made me think about it having really long legs."

"Good job, Sally. Writers carefully craft phrases—sometimes with rhyme, rhythm, or alliteration—to help readers focus on just one part of the picture."

As students share their observations, I take notes on our mini-lesson chart:

Writers help readers visualize the text.

- Use comparisons to everyday things
- Use catchy phrases with rhyme or alliteration to catch the reader's attention
- Include colors if it's important to the topic
- Include small details you don't want readers to miss—like the hairs on the spider's legs

"This is a good start to our list," I say. "As you read and write, you might notice other ways to help readers visualize your writing. We can add your ideas to the chart.

"In your notebook, focus on creating images for your reader. Turn to the next clean page. I want you to think about a part of your topic you really want your reader to visualize. If you're writing about snakes, you may want to focus on how they move. Or if you're writing about life during the Civil War, you might want to focus on the kind of clothing they wore. Take a moment to think about one small part of your topic and write that at the top of your page. Then turn and talk to your partner about your plan."

I give students a moment to talk, and when they are ready, we continue.

"Now, I'd like you to take a few minutes and try to write about your idea in a way so that readers can visualize it. You might try comparisons, catchy phrases, colors, or small details. Try to write quickly and to find as many ways as you can to create the image in your mind with words on your page."

The students begin to write. Some think for a moment and then begin to write. Some make lists of phrases, others write in sentences. A few doodle first to get their idea down and then write. After a few minutes, I stop them and ask them to share with their partner two things they tried.

I lean in to listen.

"I'm writing about Bigfoot," begins Emily. "I want my readers to picture how scary Bigfoot would be to see in real life. I wrote: 'as tall as a big tree, hairy like a gorilla, and big feet the size of a cookie sheet.'"

"Wow," replies Michelle, her partner. "A cookie sheet is huge for feet! I can fit three or four of my feet on a sheet, I think. I might have to try that at home."

I let Michelle and Emily finish sharing and listen in on other students. Then I wrap up the mini-lesson.

"Boys and girls, you're doing a great job. How many of you have a picture in your mind based on your partner's writing?"

Hands go up.

"Great. Today you can continue doing this in your notebook to generate different ways you can create images for your piece. When you write something that works well, you can add it to your draft."

And off they go.

* * *

"Creating images" is a strategy that can be easily overlooked when you're in a hurry. Yet, it's an important part of the writing process. Students need to look at other writers' work to understand the impact strong details make in an informational piece. This strategy gives students time to get interesting phrases and details down in their notebooks that they can later use in a draft. Here is a list of some of my students' big topics, images, and quick lists.

snakes—their eyes—no lashes, no eye lids, filmy cover like contact lenses to keep dirt out—always watching, always awake, always aware *(Towner, age 8)*

Big Foot—scary looks—big as a tree; hairy like a gorilla; feet the size of cookie sheets; yellow hungry eyes; steak knife sharp teeth with drool coming out of his mouth; hairy hands that need a manicure *(Emily, age 9)*

black holes—what they look like—nothing, a black splat in space, like an oil puddle on your driveway at night, it's like a ghost—you can't see it but you know it's there, camouflaged traps for stars *(Everett, age 9)*

black holes—what they do— hungry, hungry holes eats everything in sight, a bottomless pit like my brother, slurp up light—crunch on stars—eats everything in sight—even Mars *(George, age 9)*

Six-Word Summary

The book *Not Quite What I Was Planning: Six-Word Memoirs by Writers Famous and Obscure* (Fershleiser and Smith 2008) is an amazing collection of people's thoughts about their lives written in just six words. This book made me think that these six words were like a summary of sorts. Knowing that Steve Moline (2012) encourages kids to recompose what they learn, I adapted the six-word memoir into a six-word summary for student research. In doing this, I found that students needed to work like poets; they had to choose their words very carefully, because they only had six. Through this process, students found they were crafting phrases that they wanted to use in their writing. In the example that follows, Zach lists several six-word summaries. Each line is a summary for his topic, the solar system. Yet, when put together, they almost sound like a poem. This was just a lucky break for him. His focus was to come up with six words to capture the solar system as a way to develop interesting language for his draft.

> the solar system
> planets dancing around the sparkling sun
> planets, asteroids, comets, and one star
> the sun – the star of it
> sun pulls the planets to orbit
> Sparkly star stays stuck in space *(Zach, grade 4)*

Strategy: Finding the Right Beginning

In his classic book on teaching writing, *What a Writer Needs*, Ralph Fletcher (1992) dedicates a whole chapter to beginnings. He says, "It is less important for a writer to find a sensational beginning than to find the *right* beginning, the appropriate lead for that article or story" (83). How true this is and how often we forget that the right beginning for each piece isn't the same for each writer.

I noticed that my own students got the idea of a grabber lead when they wrote narrative pieces. However, for some reason, when writing informational pieces, they often reverted to stale, basic beginnings. "I am writing all about football." Or "Hi! I'm Aimee and I'm going to tell you about rabbits." I had to stop and reflect on how I taught students about beginning informational pieces. When I saw those stale beginnings time and time again, it must have been me—right? *Right.*

I discovered that I wasn't discussing beginnings with my students as we moved toward informational pieces. I assumed that they would hold on to what they knew about narrative writing and would apply it to informational writing. Yet, that's just not how kids think. Many of my students saw informational pieces as totally separate from narrative pieces, yet they are linked by the qualities of good writing. It was my job to help them see this by teaching it explicitly. And, I started at the beginning.

"Writers, would you please gather around with your notebooks and pencils?" I say as the children transition into the writing workshop. "We've been thinking a lot about writing an informational article. I think most of us have our topics and angles ready to go, right?"

Students nod their heads—a bit sleepily with the rainy day outside our window. "I'd like you to turn to your partners and tell them what your topic and angle are for your piece," I say. I give the kids just a couple of minutes to chat about their work. This helps bring them back to life and to refresh their own memory of where they are in the writing process.

"Okay, today we're going to focus on beginning our articles," I say.

Everett raises his hand. "I already started my piece," he says. Others begin to nod.

"Perfect. Writers often start their articles or other writing and get their ideas down. Then they go back to look at how they can strengthen their work. We call that . . ." I pause.

"Revision," Everett dutifully says.

"Right. But some of our friends in class haven't started their drafts yet, and it's okay to think about your beginning as you start to write, too." I want kids to understand that this lesson isn't about where they are in the writing process; it's about writing a solid beginning. This work can be done with any kind of writing during any part of the writing process.

"Today I'm going to give you some different kinds of texts to read. Some of you will get an article, and others will get a book. I'd like you to read the beginning of the article or book with your partner. Then, talk about how the writer started the piece. Let me show you what I mean."

I use my interactive whiteboard to show the students the beginning from the article "Great Migrations: Move as Millions, Survive as One," by Daphne Liu:

Hooves pound. Wings beat. Fins paddle. Every year, millions of animals move across Earth. Guided mostly by instinct, some travel thousands of kilometers, others hundreds of meters. No matter how far the journey, all face great danger.

Why do they go? They migrate in search of warmer weather, food, or safe places to raise their young. They migrate to survive. Join some of nature's greatest travelers as they make extreme journeys across air, land, and sea. (2010, 3)

I read the beginning aloud to my students. Then I pause and say, "I really love this beginning. What do you think?"

Emma speaks first. "I like the action in the beginning."

"Yeah," George adds, "and then she sneaks in some danger when she says 'all face great danger.' I wonder what kind of danger."

"Those are good observations," I say. I then use my interactive whiteboard pen to highlight the first three sentences and the phrase "all face great danger."

"It doesn't sound boring," says Everett. "It makes me think this is going to be an interesting article."

"Why? What did the writer do to grab your attention?" I ask.

"I think it's the idea that the animals have to survive. They have to move or die. That's intense," he says.

I mark the sentence "They migrate to survive."

"Writers, did you see what we did? We read a short part of the article—the introduction—and thought about what the writer did. In my notebook, I'm going to note this as an action beginning laced with danger. I could write my article with this kind of beginning, but I'm writing about ducks. My ducks aren't really in danger. So this might not be the right kind of beginning for me. I'm going to keep note of it in my notebook, though, because I may need it someday.

"Get with your partners and read the beginnings of the articles or books I gave you. You have two to read and talk about. Decide what you think the authors did in the leads and make note of your thoughts in your notebook. We'll come back together in five minutes."

Students don't need much time for this, because they're only reading a paragraph or two of each partner's article or book. Also, by the time I do this lesson, my students have worked with different kinds of leads for narratives. The goal is to help them see similar kinds of leads in nonfiction writing.

If students do not have copies to glue into their notebooks, how will they make note of the kinds of introductions they have found? Mostly my students will jot down the title and author and then describe what the author does. For the article I used with the mini-lesson, I might write this in my notebook:

> *"Great Migrations: Move as Millions, Survive as One" by Daphne Liu.*
> *NGE Nov/Dec 2010*
> *The introduction has action. She uses two-word sentences. She makes it seem dangerous.*

Then I would go on to jot down the next introduction and title. Some students may need more examples, and you can copy and trim different kinds of beginnings for kids to glue into their notebooks. Or you can have kids find "just-right" beginnings and then create a class anchor chart or bulletin board with the samples. The important thing is getting the kids to read and become familiar with the different ways writers begin informational pieces and *then* try these kinds of beginnings in their notebooks.

When I gather the students back together, we take a few minutes to discuss the different kinds of leads they've found. I then ask the students to start their writing time by trying these methods in their notebooks with their own topics.

"So today, I'd like you to take some time to tinker with your beginning. You can try an action lead like the one in the article I read. You can try a question lead like the one James found. Both you and your partner have at least two different kinds of leads that you read and talked about today. In your notebook, try them out with your topic. If you like what you write, you can move it to your draft. If you don't, we'll keep studying leads this week and we'll find the right kind. No worries. Off you go."

In Figure 5.1, I've listed some common leads I've found in nonfiction texts that I share with students. I find it's helpful to have more than one resource for these kinds of leads, so you can show students different ways authors use the same kind of writing. This list will get you started.

Figure 5.1 Kinds of Leads Used in Nonfiction

Kind of Lead	Resource(s)	How to Do It
Action	"Great Migrations: Move as Millions, Survive as One" by Daphne Liu (2010)	Use two-word sentences with active verbs to show movement.
Meet the Character	"The World's Greatest Athlete" by Joshua Cooley (2012)	Introduce the person you're writing about. Use a quick, interesting fact to launch the piece.
Meet the Characters	"Cheetah and Dog: Best Friends Forever" by M.A. Rosswurm (2012)	Describe the scene when the two characters meet.
Set the Scene	"Lively Lizards" by Lana Costantini (2010)	Describe the setting for your piece.
What It's *Not*	*Caves* by Stephen Kramer (1995)	Describe your topic by what it's not or what it doesn't have. Then tell the opposite in the next paragraph.
Over the Shoulder	"Space Quest" by Don Thomas (2011)	Write as if your reader can look over your shoulder, seeing what you see.
Being There	"Taking a Bath . . . With Friends" by Marcia Amidon Lusted (2009a) (An article about Ancient Rome)	Address the reader as *you* (use second person). Write a scene as if your reader is where your topic is taking place.
I Have a Question	*Who Would Win? Komodo Dragon vs. King Cobra* by Jerry Pallotta (2011) "Have a Toga Party!" by Marcia Amidon Lusted (2009b)	Ask a question or two that your article will answer.
Combo	*The Tarantula Scientist* by Sy Montgomery (2004)	Combine "Action," "Being There," and "Meet the Character" leads.
Narrative	"How Mosquitoes Survive in a Downpour" by Elizabeth Svoboda (2012) *There Goes Ted Williams: The Greatest Hitter Who Ever Lived* by Matt Tavares (2012)	Start with a quick narrative/story to lead your reader into your topic.

Strategy: Careful Word Choice

As teachers, we talk a lot about careful word choice. We have our students use vivid verbs and specific nouns. We want them to use details that paint pictures inside the minds of their readers. We also teach students about subject-verb agreement and pronoun antecedent agreement, among other things. Word choice is essential to writing. It *is* writing.

Somehow, with informational writing, my students tend to turn off what they've learned about word choice, and they struggle to make their pieces sound interesting. They get stuck on the idea that nonfiction means true, and so there is nothing new for them to add. The idea of crafting the piece or choosing different words than those the sources have used is difficult, because the topic was already written about and it's *true*. This is one reason I'm glad the committee for the CCSS was careful about their word choice and chose *informational writing* rather than *nonfiction*. Although informational writing is based on facts and information that is truthful, it relaxes the idea that there is only one way to write in this genre. I think this word choice, *informational writing*, gives students the opportunity to think differently about how to write "nonfiction" as well as to consider the words they'll use.

I have taught students a lot about how to paint pictures in readers' minds with words. When writing fiction, it's essential to do this so readers can follow the story and envision it in their minds. When writing informational pieces, this is important, but you also have the advantage of using visual graphics to get your point across. Graphics, however, do not always evoke emotion. So, here again, word choice is essential. Informational writers want their readers to feel something, too. They want to get their readers involved with the text to feel a part of the piece.

Day 1

I usually start this lesson by talking to the kids about how they want the reader to feel when he or she reads the piece. Do they want the reader to feel excited, scared, sad, or happy? Do they want the reader to think positively or negatively about the topic? What kind of emotion do they want to convey to the reader?

These are important questions, because writers choose words to guide their reader. The reader only knows what the writer puts on the page, not necessarily the writer's intent. It's up to writers to choose the words that will convey the kind of feeling they want for the reader.

Here's a passage from *You Wouldn't Want to Be Sick in the 16th Century! Diseases You'd Rather Not Catch* by Kathryn Senior:

Battlefield Horrors

One of the worst places to be in the 16th century is in the middle of a war. In 1563, you are officially made a barber surgeon in an army fighting in northern France. Soldiers face guns and muskets as well as swords, arrows, pikes, and axes. The injuries suffered are horrendous, and barber surgeons like you can do very little to help. Conditions are filthy, and there are no antiseptics. Limbs damaged in battle usually become infected and have to be amputated. Several people have to hold the soldier down during surgery. Even though he is given a whack on the head with the surgeon's mallet to knock him out, he will suffer tremendous pain. Few survive long after this dreadful ordeal. (2002, 14)

From the title of the book alone, readers get the feeling that the author is going to point out all the things we wouldn't like about being sick in the sixteenth century. I read the passage to my students twice—once so they can get the feel of it and the second time so they can begin marking the text. I give each student a copy of this excerpt to glue into their notebooks on the next clean page.

Before I read the text a second time, I remind the students to mark the text for words or phrases that give them a negative feeling—a feeling that being hurt on the battlefield during the sixteenth century would be a very bad thing. I reread the passage and allow kids to mark the passage as I read.

I have the students share with their partners the different words or phrases that they marked and why they chose them. When the partners are finished we gather again as a large group to share.

Here are some of the phrases or words marked and shared by students:

- *horrors**
- *worst places to be**
- *in the middle of a war*
- *guns, muskets, swords, arrows, pikes,* and *axes*
- *suffered**
- *horrendous**
- *no antiseptics*
- *limbs damaged*
- *amputated*
- *hold the soldier down*
- *whack on the head**
- *suffer tremendous pain*
- *few survive*
- *dreadful ordeal**

Some of these words and phrases are facts about war during the sixteenth century. Some of the phrases are meant to make us—the readers—feel like we are very lucky not to live during those times. As a class, we go back through our list and star the words that are not facts, but carefully chosen words to help us understand the author's point of view.

After this, my mini-lesson time is usually about over. I invite the kids to read over their writing and mark the words they're using to elicit an emotion from their reader. Because this is often something they need to work on in their writing, I'll introduce a notebook strategy in the next day's mini-lesson to help students generate words to develop the mood of their writing.

Day 2

I direct the students to look at another quick mentor text from *The Tarantula Scientist* by Sy Montgomery (2004). I ask the children to think about, as I read the text aloud, how the author wants us to feel toward tarantulas. Does she want us to be afraid or amazed? Grossed out or intrigued? I ask them to think about the feeling they get from her words as I read the text for the first time. The second time I read it, I ask the students to look for and jot down the words the author used to help them get this feeling.

> *Tarantulas are superspiders, and not just because they're so big and strong and hairy. Most spiders live only a season or two. Some tarantulas can live thirty years. And tarantulas are among the world's most ancient groups of spiders. Sam [the tarantula scientist] considers them "sort of spider dinosaurs." Tarantulas have been around for more than 150 million years—and unlike the dinosaurs, they're not extinct. They have a lot to teach us!*
> (Montgomery 2004, 13)

Many of the children notice that they were getting interested in knowing more about tarantulas. In this paragraph, they don't seem scary but rather super interesting. Here are some of the words or phrases kids picked out:

- *superspiders*—reminds me of the word *superhero*
- *world's most ancient groups of spiders*
- *spider dinosaurs*
- *more than 150 million years*
- *a lot to teach us*

I tell the students, "Just like the authors we have been studying, you too can layer your informational piece with feeling. By choosing the right words—words and phrases that will give your reader a certain feeling about your topic—you will draw your reader into your work.

"In your notebook, on the next clean page, I want you to think about how you feel toward your topic. Are you angry that people use dogs to fight? Are you worried that kids with peanut allergies don't have enough lunch choices? Are you fascinated by how a jaguar survives in the jungle? What's your feeling? Take a moment to think about that and then write briefly about it in your notebook."

I give the kids a couple of moments to do this. Then I have them turn to their partners and share what they're thinking.

"Now, I want you to generate a list of words and phrases that are about your topic and will give off the vibe that you're trying to pass on to your reader. This is similar to other notebook strategies we've used, but the purpose is to generate a feeling."

From here, students will be able to pick and choose the words or phrases that will fit with their piece. It's also a strategy that can be replicated for any kind of informational and/or argumentative piece. Being aware of the feeling or mood you create is an important part of being a writer—any kind of writer.

Here are some student examples:

George (grade 4)

Titanic—I am angry that poor people were not treated fairly, so most of them died on the ship.
• locked in—prisoners below
• left to die
• forgotten
• not included—in the women and children leaving the ship

Robert (grade 3)

Football is TOUGH.
• sweat and tears
• bruises
• pushed down over and over
• sweaty
• heavy equipment
• long practices

Hailey (grade 3)

I love my summer camp!
• fun
• friends
• laughing
• sing silly camp songs
• jump and splash

- memories
- good times
- yummy treats
- playing
- sunny

Strategy: Writing in Slow Motion

My son, Michael, plays baseball. He is what coaches call a power hitter. He can hit far and hard. He's had several batting lessons, as he is hoping for a homerun someday soon. He's getting to the fence, just not over it.

At Michael's batting lessons, his batting coach has me video record his swings. When we play back the swings, the coach slows it down so Michael can see each part of the swing. Michael can see exactly what he is doing right and when he is doing it. He can also see exactly where he needs to improve. Having this type of visual is crucial for him, as he is able to better envision what he needs to do when batting as he goes after that elusive out-of-the-park homerun.

Readers need the same kind of visual when they're trying to envision something for which they don't have the support of ample background knowledge. When writing informational pieces, it's helpful for the writer to keep this in mind. Just as in narrative writing, when we slow down the hot spot to build tension, we can slow down the "any spot" to help our readers envision our work.

Thinking about this, I turned to the article, "Swimming into History" by Debra Dragovich (2012). The article starts off when swimmer Lynne Cox was just nine years old swimming in an outdoor pool with her teammates. A storm came in, and her teammates stopped swimming, but not Lynn. She stayed in the pool. Then, to help the readers understand and visualize the severity of the storm, the writer slows down the action:

But soon the wind whipped up big waves in the pool that tossed her from side to side. Then Lynne was pelted by a hard, driving rain. Finally, she was blasted by hail the size of frozen peas.

Most swimmers would have left the pool as soon as it started raining. But Lynne stopped swimming only long enough for the hail to stop. When she continued swimming, hailstones floated on the surface of the pool. She felt as if she were swimming through a big bowl of icy tapioca pudding.

Lynne swam for three hours that day. (36)

I want to show my writers this kind of writing, because it demonstrates how a writer can show and not tell. The writer shows the storm by slowing it down—breaking it into pieces—"wind whipped up big waves," "pelted by a hard, driving rain," and "blasted by hail." She uses common foods to help students visualize the size of the hail and the feeling Lynne had swimming through the ocean. Each piece of the storm having its own sentence gives the reader time to really visualize and appreciate the severity of the storm. And it leaves me, the reader, in awe of this young swimmer.

This is the kind of writing I want from my students. When they find a place in their writing where they want the reader to truly visualize the detailed picture, it's time to slow it down and write about it piece by piece. Before my students try this in their notebooks, I share with them a sample I wrote.

"Writers, I am working on a piece that explains how to carve a pumpkin. I found it rather easy to just write the steps, but carving a pumpkin isn't easy. It's messy and you have to be strong to get through the thick shell. So, I'm going to try to slow down some of my writing in order to help the reader understand that this is not an easy task. Here's my current draft."

Next, it is time to use a carving knife to cut out the pieces you drew on your pumpkin. Use the lines you made with your pencil as a guide. Soon you will have a face on your pumpkin!

As I read, students nod and agree that the writing doesn't reflect the difficulty level of carving a pumpkin.

George says, "My dad does the carving and I watch TV. When he's finally done, I get to see it. It takes a long time."

Other kids nod their heads.

"George, you are so right! Do you know why it takes your dad so long to carve the pumpkin?" I ask.

"No. I think it's because he doesn't use the big knives much," he says.

"Writers, this is where I think I can help my readers, like George, understand how difficult it is to carve a pumpkin. While I work on it in my notebook, I want you to reread your draft. Find one or maybe two places where you could slow down your writing."

I write in my notebook as the children reread their drafts, mark the spots where they could slow down their writing, and then whisper with their partners about their plans for revision. By this time of year, we have the hang of using writing partners even without being told to do so.

"Okay, here is my first attempt at slowing down. What do you notice I'm trying to do in order to slow down this spot?" I ask. Using a document camera, I'm able to show the students my notebook work on the whiteboard.

> Now it's time to use a carving knife to cut out the pieces of your pattern. (Have a parent or adult do this part.) Carving a pumpkin isn't like slicing a turkey. You have to use short, small strokes.
>
> Slowly move the knife in and out in short back-and-forth motions. This will help you keep control of the knife and move it to the next position. The shell is thick and hard, so it will take some muscles to move the knife in and out of it. The shell doesn't move either, so when you have to move your knife over a curve or around a circle, it can be tricky. You still have to use the small back-and-forth motions. You can't just glide the knife around the pattern.

Emma volunteers some feedback first. "You wrote a lot more. You compared it to carving a turkey. I think carving a turkey would be easier."

Everett adds, "And you wrote about the back-and-forth motion. The knife can't glide. That makes me think it's hard to carve a pumpkin."

"Anything else?" I ask.

"You say the shell doesn't move and it's thick," says George.

"Yes. I'm trying to give the impression that this is a hard job—carving a pumpkin. You can't just slice through it, you have to take little strokes and move at a slow pace to get it right," I say. "In narrative writing, slowing down the hot spot means writing about every detail to build suspense or to slow the action down. We use this same technique in informational writing to show all the small parts of an action or a setting that the reader might not know.

"Now that you have found a spot or two in your draft, try writing in slow motion—step-by-step—in order to help your reader. Write in your notebook first, as you may want to try it more than once. When you think you've nailed it, share it with your partner and add it to your draft. Off you go."

Slowing down the hot spot is an important part of keeping a reader's interest. Writers break down processes or events with details to help the reader envision the event at hand. Too many details can distract the reader, but describing moment by moment once or twice in a piece can be very effective. Sometimes writers are afraid they're giving too many details. Sometimes that's true. This strategy helps students get down all the details to slow down their hot spot. If they have too many details, they don't have to use them all in the draft. See Figure 5.2 to see how one student tries to slow down her guide for sledding by giving a little more information under each guideline. Robert, in Figure 5.3, actually slows down his writing to the final seconds of his game.

Strategy: Over-the-Shoulder Writing

I admire people who can exercise at home. I admire people who can watch a video and know exactly how to imitate whatever is on the screen of their iPad or television. I also admire people who can take

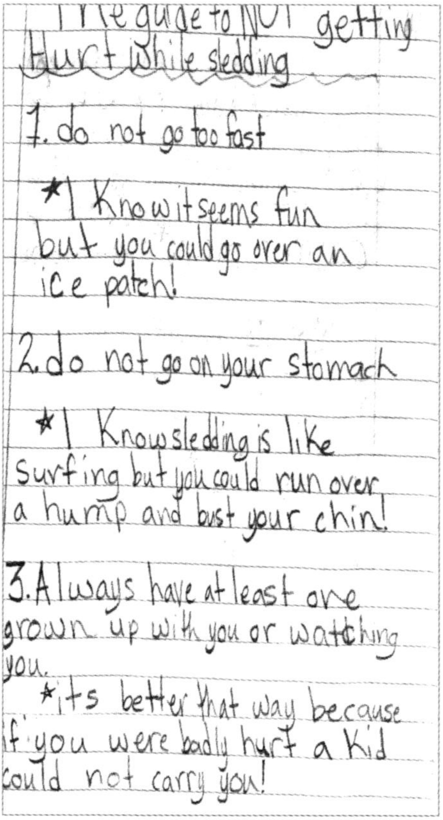

The guide to NOT getting Hurt while sledding

1. do not go too fast

*I Know it seems fun but you could go over an ice patch!

2. do not go on your stomach

*I Know sledding is like surfing but you could run over a hump and bust your chin!

3. Always have at least one grown up with you or watching you.

*its better that way because if you were badly hurt a kid could not carry you!

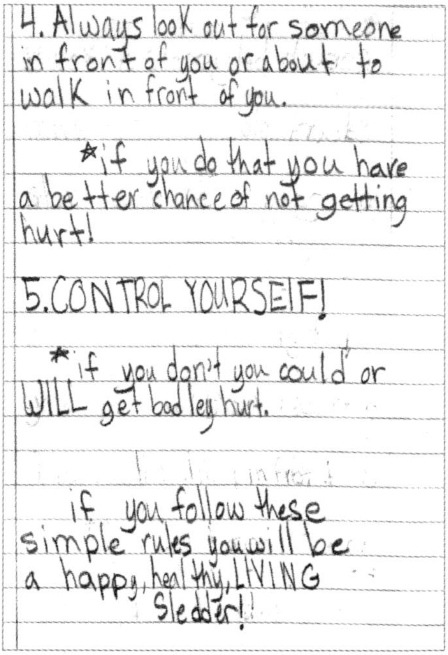

4. Always look out for someone in front of you or about to walk in front of you.

*if you do that you have a better chance of not getting hurt!

5. CONTROL YOURSEIF!

*if you don't you could or WILL get bad leg hurt.

if you follow these simple rules you will be a happy, healthy, LIVING Sledder!!

Figure 5.2 Emily, a third grader, wrote this guide for how not to get hurt sledding. Notice that she tried to develop each of her hot spots by writing a little more under each item. Before she moves back to her draft, she may want to lift one of those lines and write more about it for further development.

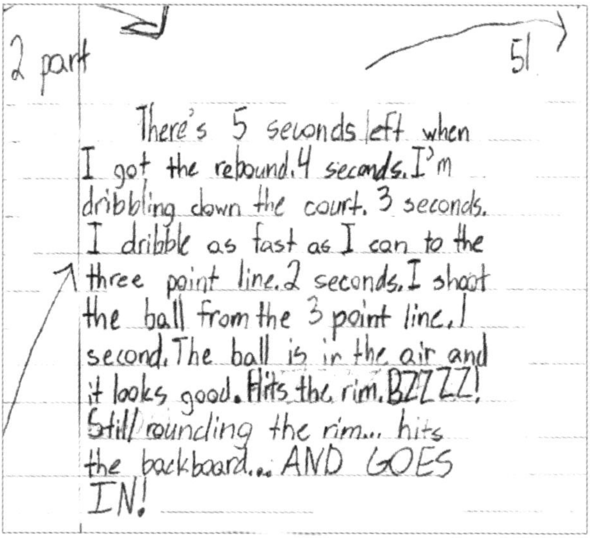

2 part   5!

There's 5 seconds left when I got the rebound. 4 seconds. I'm dribbling down the court. 3 seconds. I dribble as fast as I can to the three point line. 2 seconds. I shoot the ball from the 3 point line. 1 second. The ball is in the air and it looks good. Hits the rim. BZZZZ! Still rounding the rim... hits the backboard... AND GOES IN!

Figure 5.3 Robert, a third grader, uses time to slow down his hot spot and to give himself opportunities to develop his piece by writing what he does each second.

Zumba classes. I've tried it before, and in my head, I actually look good working out. Then I have to go past a mirror and my moves look *nothing* like what the instructors are doing. I think part of the reason this happens to me—other than because I have no rhythm—is that when I'm learning to do something new, I need step-by-step instructions.

Oftentimes, when writers are explaining something complex, they forget that the readers may not have the background knowledge needed to follow their thinking. In addition, it's sometimes ineffective to try to show instead of tell in writing so that readers can envision something complicated. In several informational books and magazine articles, I've noticed that writers use pictures with captions to help readers follow a complex process or to slow down a process for readers to see step-by-step. It's almost as if readers are able to look over the writer's shoulder and really see what he or she means.

In his book *I See What You Mean: Visual Literacy K-8*, Steve Moline explains why it may be best for the reader if the writer uses a different kind of text to communicate the information.

Students need opportunities to learn when one kind of text is better for their writing purpose than another. Suppose we want to explain the difference between an insect and a spider. Shall we draw a diagram of each? Or summarize the differences in a table? If we use diagrams, we can see the differences of shape and position as well as the number of parts. All these things define what makes an insect or a spider. But we have to go searching for those differences, detail by detail. On the other hand, if we use a table we can match up those differences under headings—number of legs, number of eyes, and so on. This helps us focus on the differences. But then, if we summarize the same information as a Venn diagram, we can focus on the similarities. Each visual text will bring some details to the foreground and obscure others. By noticing these unique properties of a labeled diagram, table, and Venn diagram, students become aware of how visual literacy can work for them. Students will learn to choose the best text for their purpose only if their literacy program provides both practice and explicit instruction in using a variety of kinds of texts. (2012, 11)

In his article "Going in Circles Around Saturn," Ken Croswell (2012) attempts to explain Dr. Robin Canup's hypothesis of how Saturn got its rings (see Figure 5.4).

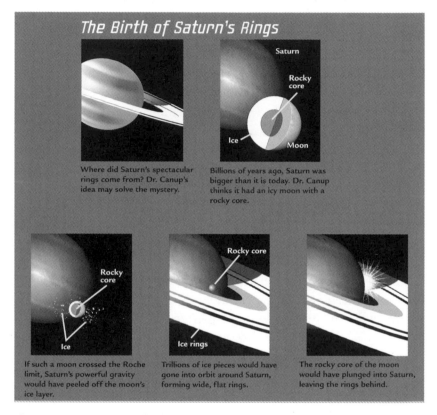

Figure 5.4 Ken Croswell uses this illustration to explain Dr. Robin Canup's hypothesis about Saturn.

Notice how the pictures and the captions go through a step-by-step explanation of Canup's complex theory. This allows the reader to follow the information with the aid of pictures to "see" what the writer (or Dr. Canup) is trying to explain. Using real photographs with explanatory captions is one way a writer can craft his or her piece to explain more clearly.

To begin this mini-lesson, I distribute copies of Figure 5.4, ready to be glued into the students' notebooks. I also have a large copy for the class to look at together.

"Boys and girls, today we're going to talk about how writers sometimes use visual representations—pictures, graphs, diagrams—to show readers what they are trying to say in their writing. Take a moment to look at the strip of pictures titled "The Birth of Saturn's Rings." Then talk with a partner about how the captions work with the pictures to explain how Saturn's rings began."

I walk around to listen to conversations, redirect those that have gotten sidetracked, and support students who are struggling. Once most of the students have had time to read and talk about this excerpt, I bring them back for a quick discussion.

"What did you learn?" I ask.

"Saturn's rings used to be a part of a moon," Robert replies.

Michelle adds, "It was the icy part of the moon that formed the rings. The rocky part of the moon crashed into Saturn."

"Why didn't gravity pull in the icy parts?" George asks.

"Good question, George. Notice how the pictures and captions give a quick summary of how Dr. Canup thinks Saturn's rings were formed. We still have questions, like George's, so we'd have to read the article. Why do you think the author used these pictures and captions instead of just relying on the words in the text?" I ask.

"Sometimes I don't look at the pictures," admits Emma, "but this gives a quick summary of what he's talking about. So it is probably good to look at before reading the article."

"Okay, so a writer might use this type of graphic to preview the information with the readers. Any other ideas?" I ask.

Haley raises her hand. "I needed the pictures to figure out what he was talking about. The words in the caption were confusing without the pictures. The pictures alone wouldn't mean much to me."

"Very interesting, Haley. I'm sure you're not alone in thinking that this article might be a bit confusing. Writers can use pictures or other visual representations to help their readers visualize what they're writing about in the article. Have any of you felt this way? You're reading a book and you have no idea what the book is saying?"

Hands go up.

"This happens a lot with informational books, especially if you don't have a great deal of prior knowledge. Using sketches, pictures, diagrams, and even maps can really help your readers. Today, I want you to think of a place in your writing where readers might be confused. Readers might be confused because you're describing something they don't know a lot about, or they might be confused because you're trying to write about something very complex. Take a moment and just think of a place in your writing where this could happen."

I give the students some time to think, and then I return to the lesson. "Today, I want you to take some time to draw some sketches and write captions to help readers visualize the part of your writing that might be confusing."

"That's it?" asks Emily.

"Yes," I reply. "Try to explain something more clearly using sketches and captions. It may not take long. Since this is in your notebook, just draw a quick sketch and don't worry about detailed pictures. Do try to write specific captions. Break down your topic into parts like you see in the example, 'The Birth of Saturn's Rings.'"

When students move to a draft or a final copy, they'll need either photographs or pictures from the computer or they'll need to draw detailed illustrations on their own. In their notebooks, however, sketches are fine.

This may seem like a strategy that most students already know. They already know there should be a caption with a picture in an informational text. We teach that when we teach text features. However, from a writer's point of view, the picture(s) chosen and the captions written are put in the piece specifically to communicate something to the reader, when words would be too much. This means that writers are not only picky about their words but also picky about the kinds of visual aids they put in their writing pieces. Everything in a piece is thought through and is there for a purpose. This stance, that the visuals are there to replace wordiness in the text, will help students take on a new sense of importance for the role of the caption.

CHAPTER 6

Assessment

August in Georgia is filled with excitement and anxiety for me. I consider this the *real* new year—new school year, new class, new school supplies, a fresh start with a world of possibilities. Yet, underlying all of this excitement is the knowledge that I'm about to get on a hamster wheel and I'll be running as fast as I can for the next ten months—running to get through the curriculum; running to administer tests for the school, county, and state; running to call parents, implement IEPs, and go to the bathroom. This running creates a level of anxiety that seems to stay with me throughout the school year until testing is over.

Assessment has become such an overused word—and action—in many schools that the word is often used in place of the word *test*. Grade-level assessments, common assessments, summative assessments, formative assessments, teacher-written assessments, textbook assessments, preassessments, end-of-term assessments, midterm assessments, and so on. Yet, we all learned in college and through our own teaching experiences that if we use assessment only at the end of a learning cycle, or only at the beginning and end, then it's really too late to help students grow.

Because We Need a Grade

With online grade books, parents and administrators are following our every move. Some of us feel pressured to have a certain number of grades entered for each grading period, whereas others of us are just happy to keep up with grading in general. The bottom line is, although writers in the real world don't get a grade, writers in school do. Grading allows us to communicate to parents and students that (1) this is important and (2) in general terms, this is how the student is progressing.

The notebook is a place to practice writing. The writing is not all going to be correct, and the writing won't always be done well. This is because I want my students to feel free to experiment in their notebooks, to plant seeds for future writing pieces, and to grow as writers. This makes grading the notebook a delicate issue. We need to assess students in order to see what they know, what they need to know, and what they're learning. A grade is one way teachers communicate to students, parents, and administrators about how students are progressing in the curriculum and achieving certain benchmarks. In the real world of writing, there are no grades on a notebook. I hesitate to show my notebooks to others, because they are filled with my practice writing, ideas that go nowhere, and spurts of inspiration. Yet, students in the upper grades do not have this luxury. Teachers across the country are being bombarded with requirements for the number of formative and summative grades they have in their grade books. In addition, with the onset of online grade books, parents are aware of the frequency and kinds of grading teachers are using to assess their children. So, with the judgment of a grade, how do we keep alive the spirit of the notebook—a place to practice and experiment with writing?

In this chapter I describe how I handle grading notebooks. There may be other ways, other rubrics, and other local requirements I don't consider in this chapter. I trust that teachers will be able to determine the best way to handle grading notebooks for their own students, even if it's not exactly how I grade notebooks.

Let's start with what I don't do. I don't go through and fix the grammar, spelling, and/or punctuation for each and every entry. I don't mark every capitalization error or make a mark where a word is obviously missing. I don't even write a comment on each entry. I preserve the notebook in its original state as much as possible. Grading is not authentic to a writer's notebook, but it is a necessary protocol. So, I try to keep them separated. There is more than enough writing in my students' lives in which to correct the use of grammar, spelling, punctuation, and other kinds of errors that I don't necessarily need to spend my time on it in the notebook.

Think about how children learn to read. Teachers and parents read aloud to them. Young readers read in small groups, with partners, and on their own. They read and read and read. But teachers don't grade and grade and grade as the children read. Rather, teachers look at the evidence over time, asking themselves, How is the student progressing as a reader, what are his or her strengths, and what lessons are needed to continue to support his or her reading growth? It's the same with notebooks. Students need to write and write and write. Teachers need to look across several entries to see how a student is progressing as a writer, determine strengths, and plan future strategy lessons.

In order to honor the idea that the notebook is a place for the writer to try things out, I don't feel it's fair to grade each page. Plus, when I'm grading twenty-five or more notebooks, the idea of traditionally grading each and every entry is overwhelming. So I look for evidence among several entries that indicates habits of mindful writing. From there, I can assess student progress with a rubric and then translate that into a grade for my grade book. In order to do all of this, I collect the notebook once or twice during a writing cycle. If my students produce three pieces during a unit of study, that means I've collected and assessed the notebook three to six times to check student progress and to determine the grade.

Formative or Summative Grade?

Many school systems are moving toward distinguishing between formative grades—grades for daily work or work that moves students toward a goal—and summative grades—tests, projects, and finals. Not only are teachers asked to distinguish between the two, but the grades are documented differently as well. With this in mind, one might wonder where to put the notebook grade. There is no one right answer here.

It makes sense to use the notebook grade as a formative grade, because the notebook is part of the progress toward writing a final piece. By checking the notebook, we're also checking on student progress toward their bigger writing project.

On the other hand, if you're looking at the notebook over the course of two weeks, it would be fair to use it as a summative grade. You're looking at how the writer managed their notebook work over the course of time. During the two or three weeks between notebook checks, you're conferring with writers and looking at their notebooks as part of your informal assessment process. So, to give it a summative grade at this point would work too.

Essentially, it comes down to what your district expects. If there are firm guidelines as to what can be a summative grade and what cannot, then you'll have to follow those. If your district requires you to have a certain number of formative grades and a certain number of summative grades, that might also push you in one direction or the other.

Habits of Mindful Writing

The whole point of *prewriting* and *revision* is to think about what one is writing and how to go about writing it well. When we draft, we're just getting down all of our ideas in a cohesive manner. Drafting is a result of all the thinking we've done during our *prewriting* stage. When we *revise*, we're reconsidering our draft. We're thinking about how to make our writing better for the reader. When we edit, we're correcting, and the final copy is just that—copying for a final clean piece. The real thinking, the real nitty-gritty work, happens in the notebook with prewriting and revision. This is why, when I assess the notebook, I try to assess from the angle that my students are developing habits of mindful writing.

What are the habits of mindful writing? If we ask five or five hundred writers, I think we'd get different answers. In order to develop my rubric, I have to think about what kind of habits I want to instill in my students with the notebook. Here are some of the questions I ask myself:

- What kind of writing are students doing in the notebook?
- What kind of evidence demonstrates that students are giving thoughtful consideration to what and how they write?
- What are good habits professional writers develop that are also in my curriculum?

- What do my students need to make a habit in order to write well after they leave my classroom?

It turns out that the answers to these questions—for me—are similar regardless of the genre my students are studying at the time. So I have one rubric for the writing notebook. It doesn't matter if we're studying narrative, informational, or opinion writing. It doesn't matter if my students are writing historical fiction, poetry, or humorous pieces. Having one notebook rubric for the whole year helps my students not only manage my expectations but also develop writing habits that transcend genre. Figure 6.1 shows the rubric I use.

Thoughtfulness

I don't pretend that this is an objective rubric. It's not. It's subjective—parts of it. The idea of being a thoughtful writer is probably the trickiest part of using this rubric. Honestly, though, I've had very little trouble with parents when I show them an entry that is thoughtful and one that is not.

Thoughtful:

I went to the beach. It was sunny and the sand was warm. The ocean's waves kept coming and going. I tried to jump over the waves, but they would knock me down. Then my big brother took my hand to wade in deeper. I was scared. He taught me to jump through the waves like a dolphin. I love being with my brother.

Not so thoughtful:

I went to the beach. We played in the water. My brother was there. It was fun.

Notice that in the first entry the writer gives some details about the setting. The writer also reveals some insights that may be new to the writer: "jump through the waves like a dolphin" and "I love being with my brother." The second entry is just a list of what happened. The

Figure 6.1 Writing Habits Across the Genres: A Rubric for Notebooks

Writing Habit	A	B	C	D
Thoughtfulness	Develops content of entries for a sense of completeness Reveals new thinking about or understanding of the topic Uses skills in GUMS* that have been mastered and explores more advanced forms of GUMS	Develops content of entries for a sense of completeness Begins to reveal new thinking about or understanding of the topic Uses skills in GUMS that have been mastered Experiments with vocabulary and punctuation not yet mastered	Some entries are complete and several are incomplete Reveals basic understanding of the topic, but does not consistently reveal new thinking Noticeable errors in GUMS that should have been mastered	Entries are too short to develop an idea or to reveal new thinking Entries are too short to demonstrate mastery of basic GUMS concepts and skills
Frequency	Has completed 90 percent or more of required entries	Has completed 80 percent or more of required entries	Has completed 74 percent or more of required entries	Has completed fewer than 74 percent of required entries
Flexibility	Maintains notes from mini-lessons Demonstrates an understanding of mini-lessons by integrating lessons into writing Tries different topics and/or modes of writing Pushes thinking by trying revision strategies more than once	Maintains notes from mini-lessons Demonstrates an understanding of mini-lessons by integrating lessons into writing Tries different topics and/or modes of writing	Maintains notes from mini-lessons Tries different topics and/or modes of writing, but only when directed to do so by the teacher	Missing notes from mini-lessons Does not attempt to use lessons to help writing Makes minimal effort toward keeping a notebook

*GUMS: Grammar, Usage, Mechanics, and Spelling

writer is recording the event rather than developing the scene. Keep in mind that for a first grader or beginning second grader, the second entry may be thoughtful and complete. As students move into third grade (and up), we need to help them develop meaningful details in their entries.

A thoughtful writer tends to write longer entries—but not always. Thoughtful writers pay attention to misspelled words, missing words, missed punctuation, and grammar functions. It's not that students are expected to reread and edit every entry before they're considered finished. However, if a student notices a misspelled word and knows how to spell the word, he or she should fix it right away. When I write and the green or red squiggly lines pop up on my computer, I fix the error immediately. I'm at a stage where I can hold my thinking long enough to do so. This is the stage we want to get our students to in their writing. We want them to be able to hold their thoughts in order to make quick fixes as they go. The bigger fixes—using new vocabulary or using apostrophes correctly—are not what I'm worried about in the notebook. I want students to practice what they know. I don't want to see the word *because* misspelled in fourth grade. I expect periods at the ends of sentences and capital letters at the beginnings of sentences. I don't expect a beginning fourth grader to use commas appropriately and consistently. That will come with time, but I do expect that of sixth graders.

As always, we must consider each student and his or her abilities. My students with learning disabilities may not spell the word *because* correctly on a consistent basis. It's important to be flexible with our grading in order to support each student's needs and to monitor each student's growth. This is probably my favorite thing about writer's notebooks: they're naturally differentiated and individualized for each and every student.

Frequency

Writers write a lot. They write often. They write and write and write. Think about how children learn to read. They read at school. They read with reading buddies. They read with their parents. Writers need practice and that's what the notebook provides—a lot of practice.

I use my grading scale for the frequency category. My scale may be different than yours. The minimal numerical grade in our school for an

A is 90 percent. I count the number of entries a student should have in his or her notebook from the last time I collected the notebook to the current time, and I hold them accountable for having at least 90 percent complete in order to earn an A. It's the easiest A one can earn; you just have to write. If students are not completing entries or are not keeping up with their work, the grade goes down. This is the most objective part of the rubric and helps balance out the more subjective parts.

Flexibility

Writers like to write what they write. And if you're being paid to write, then that's cool. If you write just for yourself, that's cool too. If you're writing for school, then you have to be a bit more flexible. Actually, all great writers learn to write by being flexible readers and writers. They read a lot of different kinds of books and they try a lot of different ways to write. This helps build a foundation from which the writer can grow. Many times people do not even know what they like until they try it.

My son is a picky eater; so much so that he doesn't like spending the night at friends' homes because he's worried he won't eat for a day. While searching online about how to solve this issue, I found that several sites recommend giving a child a new food ten to fifteen times before deciding whether they will eat it or determining that their taste buds don't like it. I'm not sure that's true, but I like the idea of it. I like the idea of giving my child steamed broccoli with seasoning one time and broccoli with a sprinkle of cheese the next. Getting my son to be a flexible eater takes work, but trying foods again and again allows him to change his mind rather than say, "I don't like it at all."

Here's the thing: if I don't keep making my son try different foods, he'll come home from college saying, "Mom! Why didn't you ever give me broccoli? I love broccoli!" (Okay, maybe not broccoli, but you get my point.) Many of my fourth and fifth graders say they hate poetry. Many times it's because they think writing poetry is writing a lot about deep feelings or having to rhyme. And let's face it, ten-year-old boys are not in touch with their feelings, and rhyming is just plain hard to do for the length of a poem. Once they try reading a variety of poems and notice they can write about sports or animals or machines and that most poetry doesn't rhyme, I often have many new converts.

Writers have to be flexible—to try new strategies, to rewrite and delete scenes, and even to explore using new vocabulary or sentence structures. This is the flexibility I'm looking for when I read my students' notebooks. Are they mixing it up? Are they writing about the same topic but from different angles? Are they writing about different topics? How are they pushing themselves as writers?

FAQ

Over the years teachers have asked me some great questions about how I assess writing notebooks.

Do you give one overall notebook grade or a separate grade for each section of the rubric?
I give one overall grade. I look at where the student is at on the rubric and then do a quick average. It's what I do, but you can also give three separate grades if you want. You don't have to give a grade at all; you could just use the rubric as a guide for giving feedback.

Do I have to use these categories: thoughtfulness, frequency, and flexibility?
Absolutely not. This is what works for me. I want to keep things simple, so I worked to create one rubric that I can use all of the time. If you read my first book, *Notebook Know-How: Strategies for the Writer's Notebook* (2005), you'll see the rubric is very similar. I change the rubric as my understanding of teaching writing changes. Each teacher needs to decide what he or she wants students to get out of using a writing notebook. You may also want to consider your school's curriculum objectives and/or the CCSS. Then you can determine the appropriate categories.

How do you grade several entries at once?
I read the section of the notebook that I'm assessing. I then reread it with the rubric in mind—looking for evidence to support my assessment. Then I mark the rubric—not the entries.

What if I want to write a comment about an entry?
There are times I, too, want to respond to an entry in writing. Maybe the student wrote about losing a loved one or celebrating an accomplishment.

I allow myself to write a short comment on the bottom of the rubric. I keep the rubric to a half-sheet of paper and I write in the bottom margin. I have also been known to write on a sticky note. If I have a full blank page near an entry, I do not write on it. Otherwise, I'll fill that page and feel guilty I didn't write as much to the other kids. I will be writing in notebooks my whole weekend, and I will lose valuable family time and/or valuable planning time. Keep assessment manageable. Giving written feedback is smart, but remember that the most frequent feedback will likely be in your conferences with students.

I teach second grade. Should I grade their notebooks?
Students should not start keeping notebooks until they are developmentally ready. They need to have the fine motor skills and knowledge of how to write on the lines. They need to be able to see entries as seed ideas and not necessarily complete stories in and of themselves. Many second graders still need to work with story maps and paper books. That being said, if your second graders are using a writing notebook and it's working for you, then no, I would not *grade* their notebooks with this rubric. They're still at an age where they need to be encouraged and celebrated with every single step. They haven't developed their abstract thinking enough to think about earning a grade over time rather than for one story at a time. I encourage you to read their notebooks and give encouraging feedback. If you absolutely must determine a grade, you will be able to develop a more appropriate rubric than the one I present here.

* * *

In the following sections, I look at two students' notebook entries over the course of a couple weeks. You'll notice the different topics the students write about, the strategies they try, and how their topics begin to take shape. My comments on the student samples consider the rubric and how I would assess these notebooks. If teachers were to change the rubric to meet their specific needs, they could use the rubric and these samples to practice assessing.

Taking a Closer Look: Raya

Raya is a fourth grader in Forsyth County Schools, Georgia. She's in Ms. Mundt's class, and they are writing informational pieces. Raya's notebook is filled with different strategies to help her think through the prewriting stage of the process.

As I read through Raya's first entry, I notice that she tries two different strategies to brainstorm a topic. She uses the "topic legs" strategy and she has a list of topics she knows a lot about (Figure 6.2).

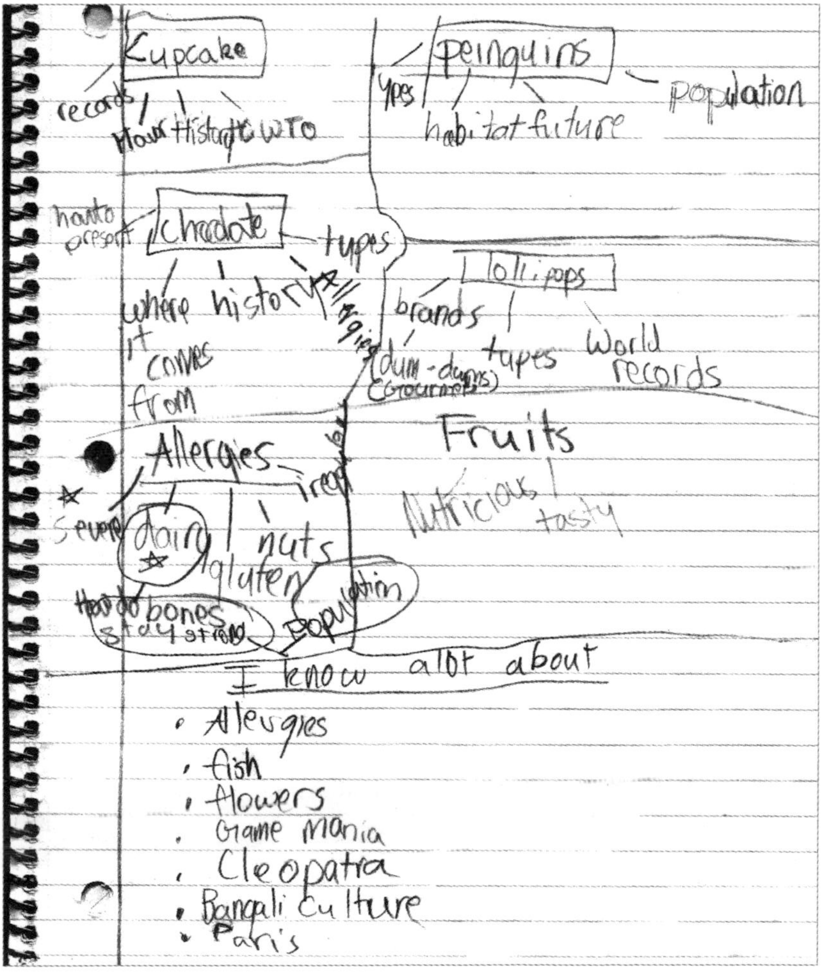

Figure 6.2 Raya's Strategies for Brainstorming Topics

The next two entries show her writing about allergies from different angles. In Figure 6.3, she writes about dairy allergies, and in Figure 6.4 she explores the idea of severe allergies.

I also notice that she is writing questions in the margins to track her thinking and to remind her of what she doesn't know about her topic. These are questions she'll need to answer with her research.

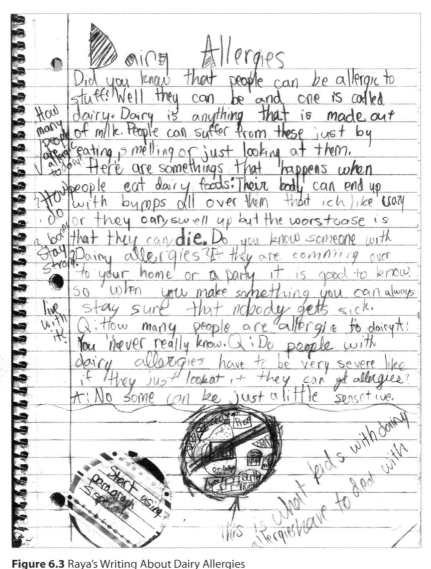

Figure 6.3 Raya's Writing About Dairy Allergies

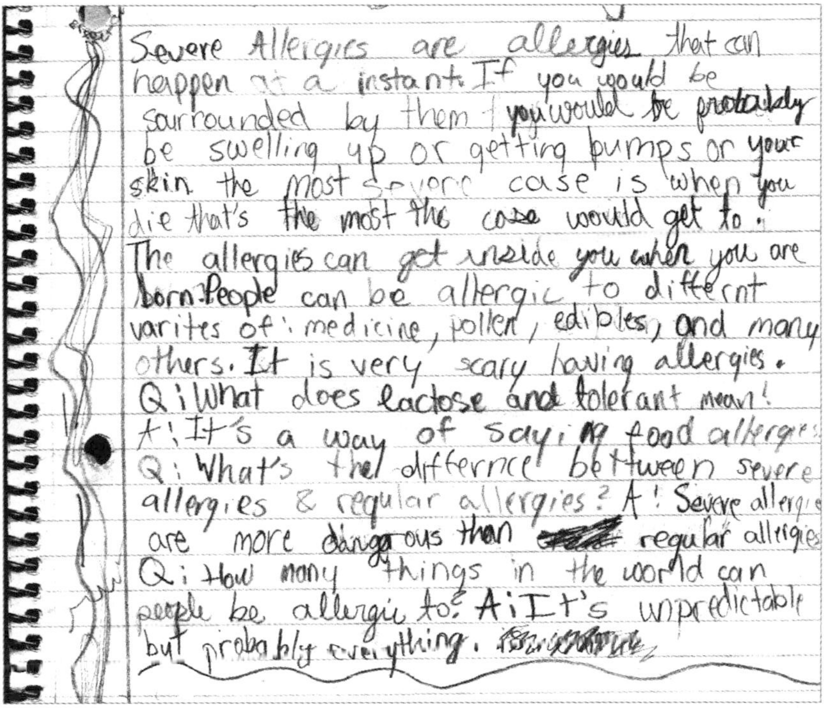

Severe Allergies are allergies that can happen at a instant. If you would be sourrounded by them you would be probably be swelling up or getting bumps or your skin the most severe case is when you die that's the most the case would get to. The allergies can get inside you when you are born. People can be allergic to different varites of medicine, pollen, edibles, and many others. It is very scary having allergies. Q: What does lactose and tolerant mean? A: It's a way of saying food allergies. Q: What's the difference bettween severe allergies & regular allergies? A: Severe allergies are more dangaous than regular allergies. Q: How many things in the world can people be allergic to? A: It's unpredictable but probably everything.

Figure 6.4 Raya's Writing About Severe Allergies

By the time Raya gets to her heart entry, shown in Figure 6.5, she has decided to write about dairy allergies because people can die from them. Raya also mentions that this allergy hurts, people suffer, and they have to be careful. Her heart reflects a new understanding about allergies—it's not just about her and her allergies. Some people have worse reactions than she does. This is a thoughtful insight.

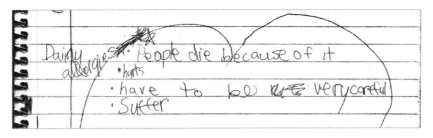

Dairy allergies: People die because of it
• hurts
• have to be very careful
• Suffer

Figure 6.5 Raya's Heart Entry

Figure 6.6 shows some of Raya's research notes. I notice she is using some strategies for recomposing what she is reading on the Internet. She uses a flowchart and pictures to help her track facts that she would like to use in her piece. From the bit of writing at the bottom, I see Raya's attitude toward allergies softening a bit. She is no longer ready to tell people how you can die from allergies, but rather that it is possible to live with dairy allergies.

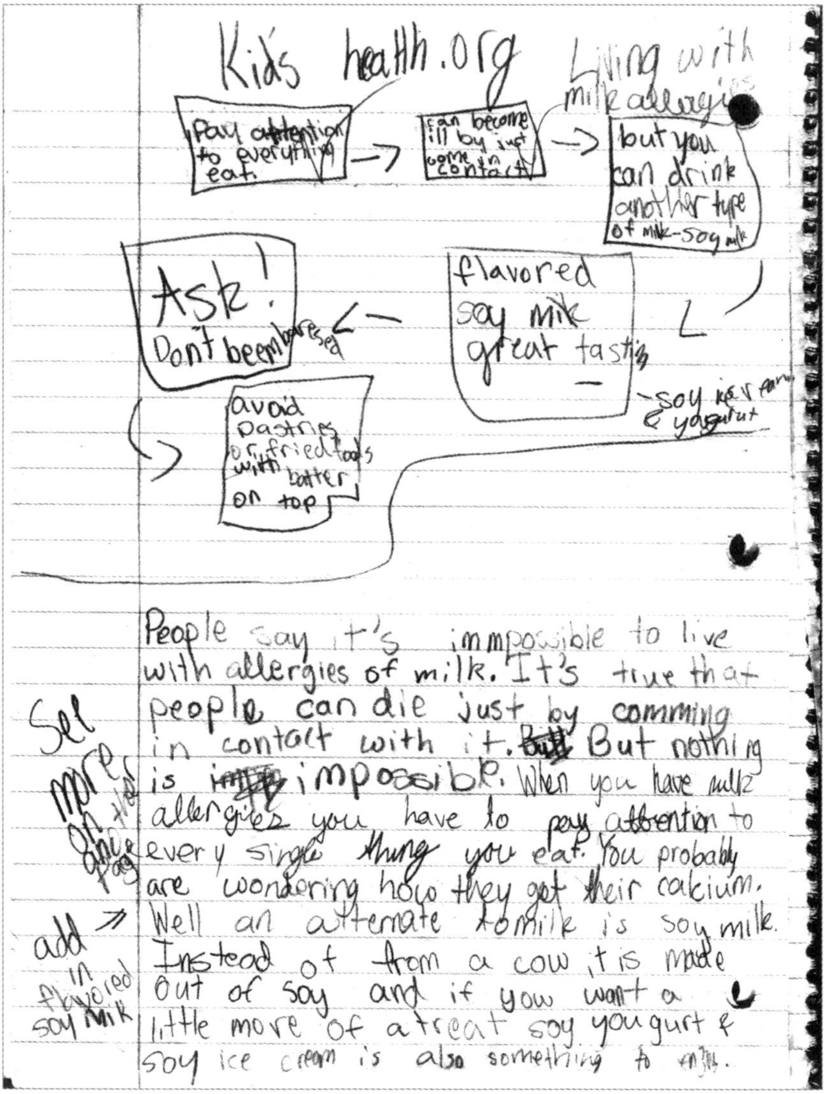

Figure 6.6 Raya's Research Notes

Overall, I can see that Raya is developing as a thoughtful, flexible, and frequent writer. She develops insights throughout her entries. She tries different angles and uses strategies she learned from mini-lessons to help her find a topic and to gather information about her topic. Raya is reflective, as we see through her questions and notes in the margins as well as a lone sticky note encouraging herself to use paragraphs. In general, she has a good handle on grammar, usage, mechanics, and spelling (GUMS). There are a few errors, but overall, she is solid in this area. She isn't necessarily trying more advanced punctuation, except in the little Q and A section at the end of a couple of her entries. In these she uses a colon to separate Q from the question and A from the answer.

Taking a Closer Look: Noah

Noah is a fourth grader in Forsyth County Schools, Georgia. He is in Ms. Mundt's class, and he is preparing to write an informational piece. Noah has kept class notes, tried different strategies, and allowed his thinking about his piece to evolve.

Like Raya, Noah begins his prewriting work with the "topic legs" strategies (see Figures 6.7 and 6.8). Noah's topic legs actually look more like webs. I can see how he connects subtopics with lines and he stars his obvious love of combat. He does not finish the strategy by writing a bit about some of these topics to try them out. His next entry moves into a list of ways writers write informational pieces (Figure 6.9).

As I continue to read Noah's entries, I can see that he is thinking about his topic. Figure 6.10 shows him planning a book on weapons, complete with page numbers and topics per page. He then tries out a top-ten list modeled after Steve Jenkins's (2009) work. So, I know he is reading informational books and thinking about different ways he could write about his topic.

Figure 6.11 shows some of Noah's first prose-like entries regarding combat. He starts with a brief history and moves into hand-to-hand combat. (Let me note that I know this is a tricky topic for most teachers in most schools. However, notice how Noah has a certain distance in his

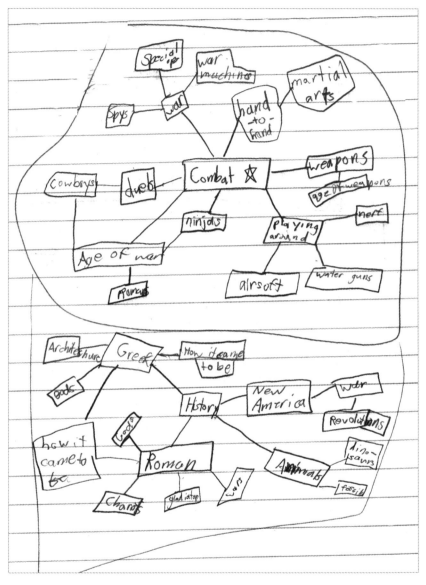

Figure 6.7 Noah's Prewriting

writing that allows him to take the stance more of an expert. He doesn't try to show rather than tell and he doesn't attempt to bring the weapons into action. This keeps the piece at an acceptable comfort level for both his teacher and me.)

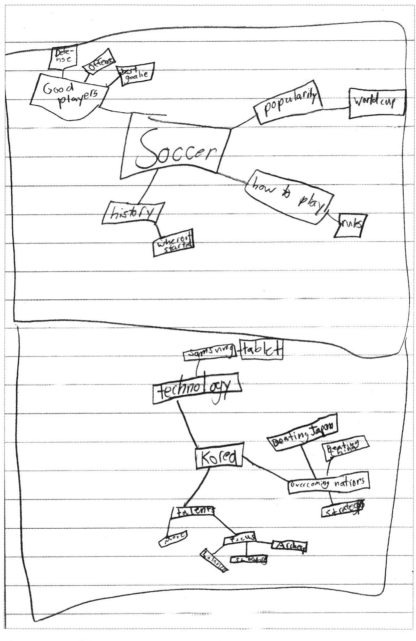

Figure 6.8 Noah's Prewriting

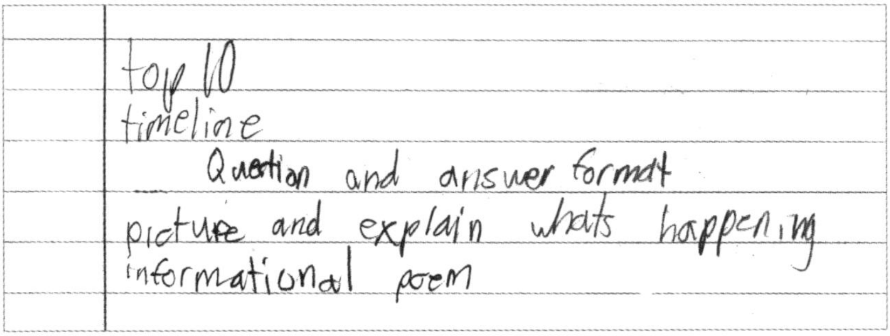

> top 10
> timeline
>   Question and answer format
> picture and explain whats happening
> informational poem

Figure 6.9 Noah's List Entry

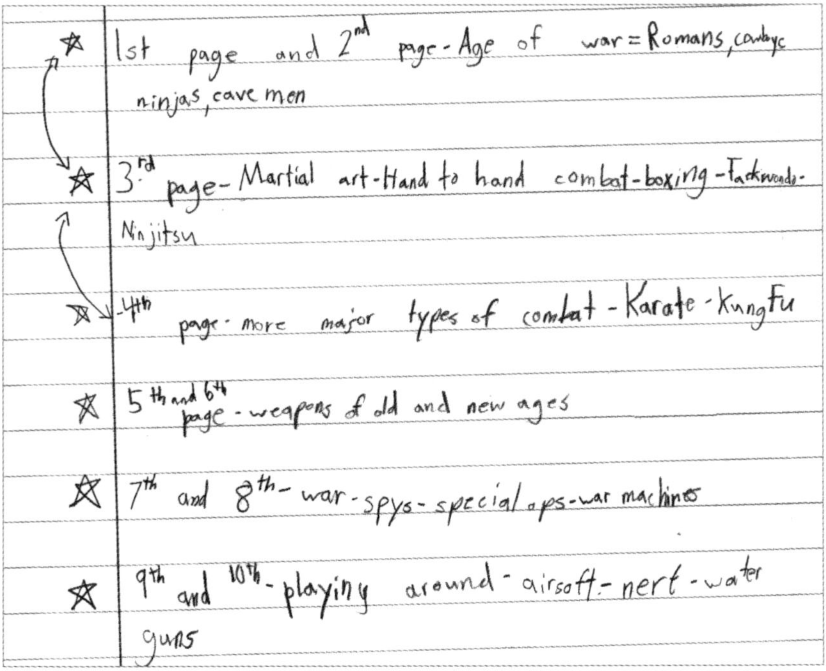

> ☆ | 1st page and 2nd page - Age of war = Romans, cowboy
> ninjas, cave men
>
> ☆ | 3rd page - Martial art - Hand to hand combat - boxing - Tackwondo -
> Ninjitsu
>
> ☆ | 4th page - more major types of combat - Karate - kung fu
>
> ☆ | 5th and 6th page - weapons of old and new ages
>
> ☆ | 7th and 8th - war - spys - special ops - war machines
>
> ☆ | 9th and 10th - playing around - airsoft - nerf - water
> guns

Figure 6.10 Noah's Planning Entry

Noah has taken notes on how to recompose using pictures. In Figure 6.12, I see his picture notes from class when we read and discussed "Living Honey Jars" from the book *Exploding Ants: Amazing Facts About How Animals Adapt* by Joanne Settel (1999). In Figure 6.13 he includes a summary of his understanding based on the picture notes he recorded in Figure 6.12.

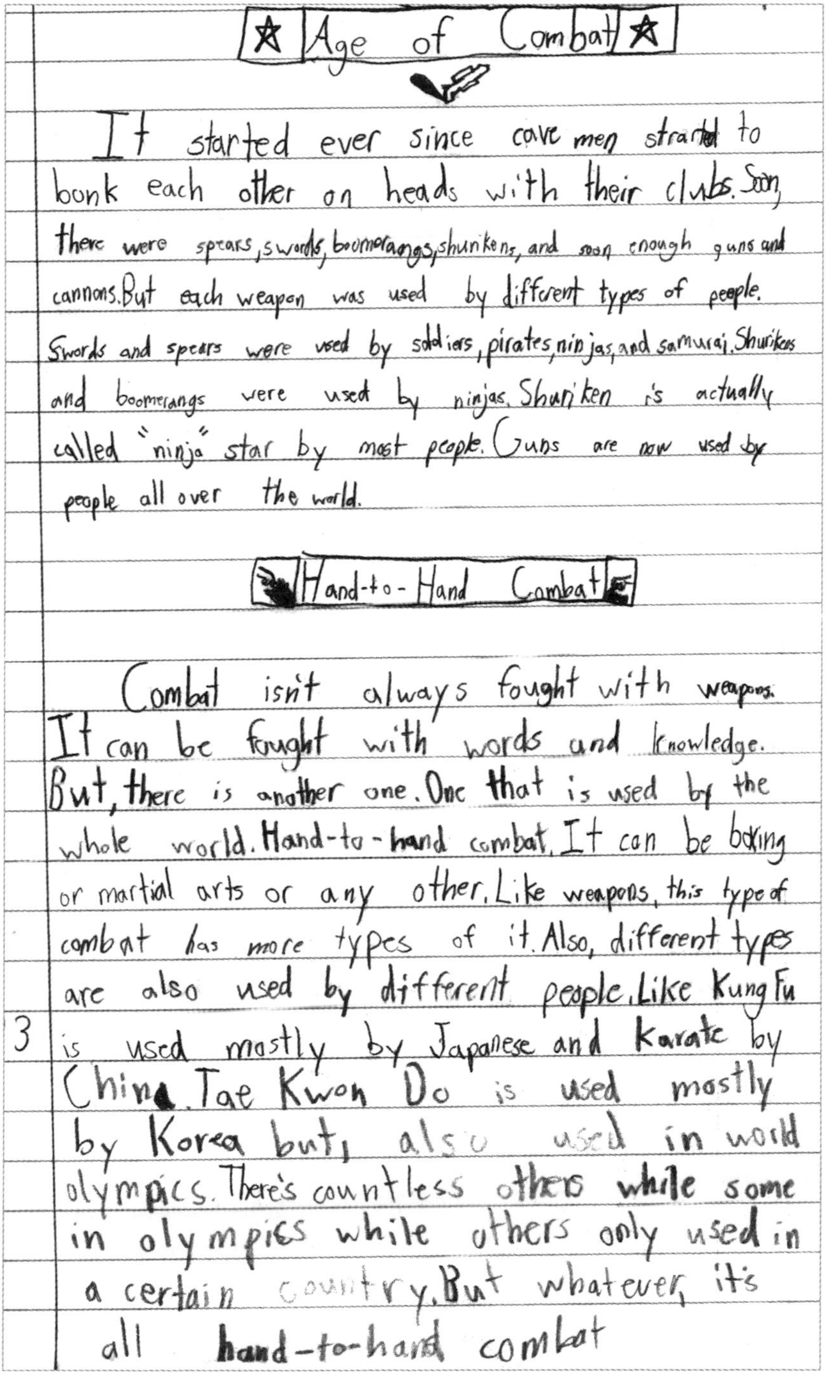

☆ Age of Combat ☆

It started ever since cave men started to bonk each other on heads with their clubs. Soon, there were spears, swords, boomerangs, shurikens, and soon enough guns and cannons. But each weapon was used by different types of people. Swords and spears were used by soldiers, pirates, ninjas, and samurai. Shurikens and boomerangs were used by ninjas. Shuriken is actually called "ninja" star by most people. Guns are now used by people all over the world.

Hand-to-Hand Combat

Combat isn't always fought with weapons. It can be fought with words and knowledge. But, there is another one. One that is used by the whole world. Hand-to-hand combat. It can be boxing or martial arts or any other. Like weapons, this type of combat has more types of it. Also, different types are also used by different people. Like Kung Fu is used mostly by Japanese and Karate by China. Tae Kwon Do is used mostly by Korea but, also used in world olympics. There's countless others while some in olympics while others only used in a certain country. But whatever, it's all hand-to-hand combat

Figure 6.11 Noah's Prose-Like Entries

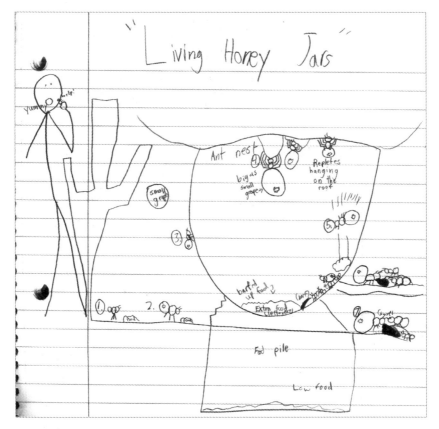

Figure 6.12 Noah's "Living Honey Jars" Picture Notes

By the time he writes the notebook entries shown in Figure 6.14, Noah has decided on his topic of machine guns and his format of a top-five list. The writing on these notebook pages integrates what he knows about his topic with new facts he's learning. Notice that under each kind of gun, he writes a bit of what he knows and then writes a bulleted note section.

Noah has a final entry about making glass (Figure 6.15). It has nothing to do with his informational piece, but it shows his flexibility with topics as well as his willingness to write beyond the workshop.

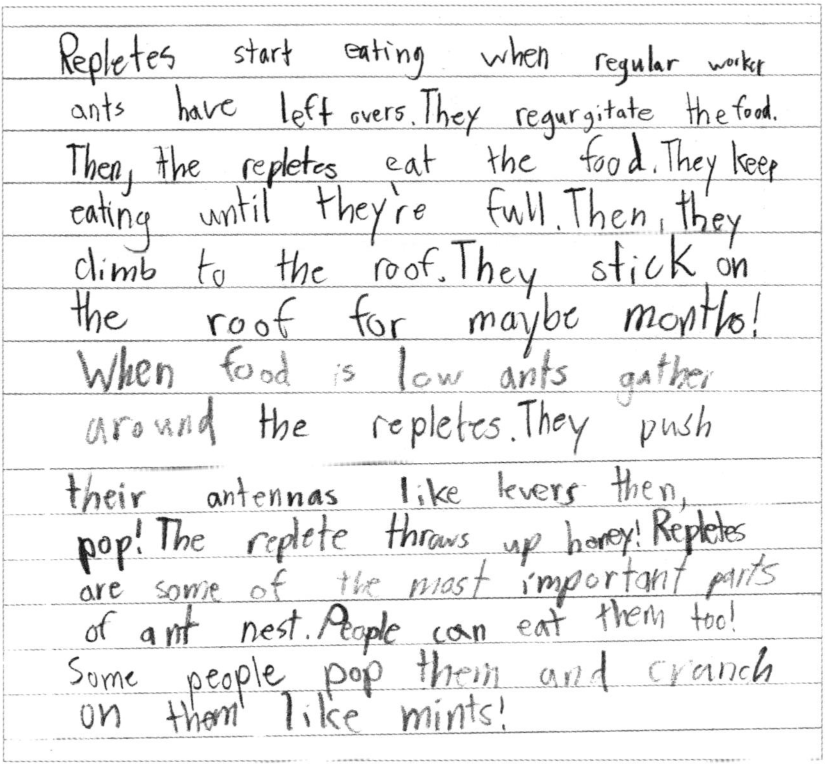

Repletes start eating when regular worker ants have left overs. They regurgitate the food. Then, the repletes eat the food. They keep eating until they're full. Then, they climb to the roof. They stick on the roof for maybe months! When food is low ants gather around the repletes. They push their antennas like levers then, pop! The replete throws up honey! Repletes are some of the most important parts of ant nest. People can eat them too! Some people pop them and cranch on them like mints!

Figure 6.13 Noah's Summary Based on His Picture Notes

Overall, Noah is also a thoughtful, flexible, and frequent writer. He does leave some strategies and entries unfinished, however. At the same time, from looking over a series of several entries, it is evident that Noah is thinking about his topic and developing his vision for his informational piece. He uses appropriate GUMS and different modes to capture his thinking.

Youtube.com
wikipedia.com

top 1 of ~~First lightest Dangerous fastest biggest~~ Machine guns   5 in all

Dangerous 1.	GAU-8 Avenger - is a 7 barrel machine gun that can shoot up to an average of 4,200 rounds per minute. It is an electric motor hydraulic driven machine gun that can shoot over 12,000 feet. It is even able to penetrate tanks.
	Notes -
	• can shoot 4,200 rpm
	• electric motor
	• hydraulic driven
	• 7 barrels
Fastest 2.	Metal Storm - Is a 36 barrel machine gun that can shoot thousands of bullets per second and one million per minute. It is controlled by a computer.
	Notes -
	• A little more than a million shots fired per minute
	• A couple thousand round per second.
	• computer controlled
Biggest 3.	40 mm Bofors - Is a fully automatic Anti-Aircraft machine gun that can shoot 150 - 200 spm (slow for a machine gun but, shoots bullets bigger than your arm. And is lever pulled.
	Notes -
	• Anti-Air craft • 5,150 kg (11,400 lb)
	• bullets bigger than arm
	• lever pulled
	• Able to blow up train in 2 shots!

Figure 6.14a Noah's Topic, Format, and Notes

Lightet 4 Madsen -

Notes
- sold to over 34 countries
- used over 100 years
- 2016 (9.07 kg)
- 450 Rounds/Min

First 5, Defense gun

Notes
- only a several revolving chambers
- Made 1718
- 1 barrel
- not successful (not used widely
- operated by hand crank

Figure 6.14b Noah's Topic, Format, and Notes

How to make Glass

Glass is created when lime from limestone, sulica from sandstone and soda are mixed together at extreme heats. Once you make glass you can make pretty china cups, nice plates and glass sculptures. Glass is used all over the world for many uses.

Figure 6.15 Noah's Entry About Glass Making

Assessing for the Next Step

Assessment isn't just about grades. Teachers who are paying attention to their students are assessing all of the time. There are two more ways teachers can assess the use of writing notebooks and how it's supporting student growth. Teachers confer with students during the writing workshop, and teachers have writing goals for each student.

It's likely most teachers are already conferring with students and setting writing goals, but we may not recognize these as informal assessments. It's important to take into account all of the ways we monitor student growth not only when report card time pops up but also when sharing student progress with parents, colleagues, and administrators. Remember, a grade or a test score is just a snapshot. We know so much more about our students, and sharing that information builds the confidence people have in us as teachers.

Conferring

I'm always surprised when teachers tell me that they don't confer with students when they are writing in their notebooks. When I ask why, teachers tell me that they don't want to interrupt the brainstorming process or that they're writing in their own notebooks or that they're too busy getting everyone on task. In the beginning of the year, these may be reasonable excuses, but after the workshop is underway and expectations are understood, the teacher needs to spend his or her time conferring while students write—even if students are writing in notebooks.

When students are working in their notebooks during the pre-writing phase, this is a key time to talk to them about developing their ideas, branching off into different topics, rereading their work to find their place in their thinking, holding ideas from one day to the next, and so on. It's also a good time to recognize which students are struggling with surface features, grammar, and spelling. Conferring during this part of the process also increases the number of conferences I can have with each student throughout the year.

So what do teachers assess when they confer? In the first few moments of a conference, I assess what the students are doing, what they've done, and what they need to do. In the following example, I'm consulting in a fifth-grade classroom. The students are all writing how-to pieces: how to play football, how to train a dog, how to get out of trouble. Mark has a huge topic: "All About Football." Like other students in his class, he struggles with writing longer entries. So, he tends to choose topics that are really big—like football—so there is more to write about in his notebook. Unfortunately, this is a common misconception. Often when kids pick such a large topic, they actually write less.

"Hi Mark," I start. "Can you find a good stopping place so we can talk?"

I wait for Mark to finish the sentence he's writing. I have noticed that when kids stop abruptly—mid sentence sometimes—it's more difficult for them to get back to their writing after the conference. As in reading, I want students to get to a good stopping place so they can easily pick up after we're through.

"What are you working on today?" I continue when Mark has stopped writing.

"I'm writing all about football. I have three parts. I'm almost done," he says proudly.

I scan his page and see that his three parts are barely full paragraphs and they take up about half his page. Not all notebook entries need to be a full page, but I do see a possible red flag when the topic is as big as football and the writing is as little as a half page. I've assessed that it's likely Mark needs help narrowing and developing his topic.

"How do you like what you've written so far?" I ask. I'm trying to get Mark to reflect on his writing to empower him to make some writing decisions to improve it.

"It's okay. I really wanted to write about quarterback plays, but my teacher said she doesn't know anything about football. I'm trying to consider my audience," he says.

"Considering your audience is important, and I'm proud of you for thinking about that. Since you're working in your notebook, it may be a little too early to be thinking about your audience. In your notebook, you're writing to explore your ideas and the best way to write about them," I explain.

Mark looks at me suspiciously. He knows I'm a consultant and that I'll be leaving. He knows his teacher will stay and isn't sure this is what she wants. I push on. "Mark, take a moment to reread what you've written. I'm wondering if there is a way you can still write about the quarterback plays."

He rereads and I take the moment to reread over his shoulder. Shaking his head, he murmurs, "I have paragraphs about rules, players, and safety. I can't fit the kinds of plays in here."

At this point, I'm thinking two things. First, I can see that Mark views his work in terms of paragraphs. Everything is a paragraph: rules, players, and safety. Second, he doesn't see how to write about the quarterback plays under the umbrella "All About Football." I decide to teach one thing—narrowing the topic to write more about it.

"Mark, sometimes writers have this problem. They're writing about a big idea, like football, and then they can't figure out how to fit in all of the little pieces they want to write about in their paper. In your case, you're having trouble writing all about football and including the quarterback plays."

He nods and looks down at his paper.

"What helps me in this situation is to try to narrow my topic and write more about just one part. I mean, people have written entire books on football! People have written entire books on just the offense, haven't they?"

He nods again. "Yeah, it's a lot," he says.

"Let's think about your big idea of football and narrow it down to quarterback plays. Is there a way you could explain what quarterback plays are to someone who is unfamiliar with football?" I ask.

His eyes seem to bulge, and he brightens as he turns to me. "Yes. I think I can just talk about the quarterback and his job in the game. That might work." He begins turning the page and picking up his pencil.

"I'm going to let you get back to work. I'll check on you later."

There are times when I look at a student's writing that I feel overwhelmed with what I need to teach the writer. I stick to this rule of thumb: Teach *one* thing in a conference. Mark's writing was littered with misspelled words and capitalization errors. Yet, I decided to teach one thing—idea development. Over time, the lessons will build up and the student will show progress. This is hard to remember when I'm faced with an entry that is underdeveloped, lacks voice, and sports weak spelling and sentence structure.

Sometimes I start with the easiest thing. For example, if I'm in a fourth-grade classroom and I notice that a student isn't using periods, my teaching point may be reminding her of why ending punctuation is important. I may even ask her to take some time and reread a couple of entries to add ending punctuation. Then I'd tell her that writers use what they know as they go to keep their writing as clean as possible. This is an easy fix. If by fourth grade a student is not using periods, it is *usually* due to a bad habit rather than not knowing when or how to use a period. A quick fix-up lesson is probably all that student needs. But notice, I wouldn't reteach the period and then talk about developing the scene and writing longer entries. I taught the idea that *writers use what they know as they go* (thoughtfulness). I want students to make minor edits as they write whenever they write.

Though I sometimes teach the easiest thing in a conference, other times I teach something that I know I'll have to return to more than once. For example, I may be working with a sixth grader and notice that he's using a lot of adjectives to make his sentences longer and to add details. I know that there are many different strategies that writers use to move away from this kind of writing. I'm not going to teach all of those strategies in a conference. I'm going to choose one that the student can manage, teach it, and then look in his notebook to see if he tried it.

When I confer with students while they're working in their notebooks, I do expect that they'll try out what I've taught them. It's not an option not to do so, and it is part of how I grade the notebook. I like students to have some experience with the strategy I'm teaching them, and I want them to have that experience right away. Students don't have to use the strategy over and over if it doesn't work for them, but they do have to try it (flexibility).

Setting Goals

When I first started teaching, I kept a lot of notes on each conference so I wouldn't forget anything. This helped me plan but also gave me talking points during parent conferences. I fretted that parents would question me and criticize me for not using a textbook, so my notes became my research on each and every student. As I became more experienced, I found that I could remember a lot of what I was doing with my students. I wrote down less. I got away with it for a year or two, but I missed out on a lot of teaching points, because I didn't write things down.

Now I've streamlined my conference notes. I tend to jot down my notes after each conference. So while the student gets back to writing, I take a moment to jot down on a template what we talked about, what I noticed, and what I taught (see Figure 6.16). I also make note if this child needs to be a part of a small group or if I need to do a whole-class mini-lesson.

Figure 6.16 Sample Conference Note Page

Date	Writing Topic	What Did I Notice?	Teaching Point	Whole Group (WG) or Small Group (SG)?
9/12	Notebook: all about football	Short paragraphs Topic too big Misuse of capital letters	Narrow topic to write more	WG: narrow topic SG: Quick reminders about capital letters

Name of student: Mark
Goals for student:
1. Come up with own topics for writing.
2. Learn to develop entries so they're longer than a half page.
3. Use varying sentence structure to add variety in work.

During my conference, I'm looking at this note template, not writing on it. I write on this page *after* the conference, when things are fresh in my mind. I'm also reviewing the notes I took the last time I conferred with the student and reviewing the writing goals I had already set. My goals for students are reminders to me for my teaching points. Notice that my conference touched on two of my goals for Mark. First, I wanted to support his attempt at coming up with his own ideas for writing: the quarterback plays. I also wanted to push him to write more than just the few sentences (what he called paragraphs) he had on his page. So, by helping him narrow his topic to write about the quarterback plays, I was able to accomplish both tasks. This doesn't mean his goals are accomplished. When I collect his notebook to assess it, I'll look for evidence that he's consistently coming up with his own (manageable) ideas. I'll look for entries that are consistently about a page long. I'll also look more closely at two or three entries to notice his sentence structure. Once I see consistent evidence that he's doing one or all of these things, I'll take off that goal and write a new one based on what his needs are as a writer. Although these goals aren't necessarily measured with a test score or a specific grade, they do help me continually assess where my students are in their growth as writers.

It's important to note that sometimes my conferences do not touch on any of the documented goals for that student. Students may have a more pressing issue with their writing at the time of our conference. I expect the writer to drive the conference, but if I need to, I use the goals to help guide their thinking.

Being Accountable

Many districts are implementing—or have implemented—rigorous teacher evaluation guidelines. Many teachers are upset, because for decades their administrators came in once a year to watch a lesson. They might get an individualized note about what was going well, but more likely they found a form in their box that said they were doing fine and please sign here.

Now, teachers are being held accountable with more rigorous evaluations. Evaluations may include a set of goals, test scores, and portfolios. Administrators are visiting classrooms for more than one lesson and often have a checklist of things they're looking for during their stay.

I mention this to remind us that our students are feeling the same way. We're constantly giving them checklists and rubrics. We're writing them notes telling them what to improve and how to do it. We create portfolios of their work and expect them to add to the portfolios on a regular basis. It's stressful.

Assessing the notebook should be a celebration of what students are trying in their writing. It's a time when I'm looking at the possibilities for each writer and trying to figure out how to get him or her there. It's about accomplishing small steps toward becoming a better writer and a better teacher of writing. Because the notebook is the practice place for writing, I expect mistakes. I expect kids will try using new vocabulary or longer sentence structure, and it may or may not work. I'm looking for evidence of growth, not necessarily for what students are doing wrong. There will always be opportunities to tell students what's wrong with their work. We have to make opportunities to show students what they're doing well. One of my goals as a writing teacher is to make notebook checks opportunities for the kind of feedback kids are eager to get.

REFERENCES

Anderson, Laurie Halse. 2002. *Thank You, Sarah: The Woman Who Saved Thanksgiving*. New York: Simon and Schuster for Young Readers.

Bragg, Georgia. 2012. *How They Croaked: The Awful Ends of the Awfully Famous*. New York: Walker.

Brown, Don. 2008. *Odd Boy Out: Young Albert Einstein*. Boston: Houghton Mifflin.

Buckner, Aimee. 2005. *Notebook Know-How: Strategies for the Writer's Notebook*. Portland, ME: Stenhouse.

Calkins, Lucy. 1986. *The Art of Teaching Writing*. Portsmouth, NH: Heinemann.

———. 2003. *Units of Study for Primary Writing*. Portsmouth, NH: Firsthand/Heinemann.

Calkins, Lucy, Marjorie Martinelli, Ted Kesler, Cory Gillette, Maria Colleen Cruz, Medea McEvoy, Mary Chiarella, and Kathy Collins. 2006. *Units of Study for Teaching Writing, Grades 3–5*. Portsmouth, NH: Firsthand/Heinemann.

Calkins, Lucy, and Leah Mermelstein. 2003. *Launch a Primary Writing Workshop: Getting Started with Units of Study for Primary Writing*. Portsmouth, NH: Firsthand/Heinemann.

Cherry, Lynne. 2013. *A River Ran Wild: An Environmental History*. Columbus, OH: Zaner-Bloser.

Common Core State Standards (CCSS). 2012. "Research to Build and Present Knowledge." English Language Arts-Literacy-Writing Standards, Grade 4. www.corestandards.org/ELA-Literacy/W/4.

Cooley, Joshua. 2012. "The World's Greatest Athlete." *Highlights for Children* 67 (10): 24–25.

Costantini, Lana. 2010. "Lively Lizards." *National Geographic Explorer*. September: 2–5.

Croswell, Ken. 2012. "Going in Circles Around Saturn." *Highlights for Children* 65 (5): 40–41.

Dragovich, Debra. 2012. "Swimming into History." *Highlights for Children* 67 (10): 36–37.

Duffey, Betsy. 2000. *The Gadget War*. New York: Viking.

Fershleiser, Rachel, and Larry Smith. 2008. *Not Quite What I Was Planning: Six-Word Memoirs by Writers Famous and Obscure: From Smith Magazine*. New York: HarperPerennial.

Fleischman, Sid. 2006. *Escape! The Story of the Great Houdini*. New York: Greenwillow.

Fletcher, Ralph J. 1992. *What a Writer Needs*. Portsmouth, NH: Heinemann.

Fletcher, Ralph J., and JoAnn Portalupi. 2001. *Writing Workshop: The Essential Guide*. Portsmouth, NH: Heinemann.

Hall, Donald. 1994. *I Am the Dog, I Am the Cat*. New York: Dial for Young Readers.

Harvey, Stephanie. 1998. *Nonfiction Matters: Reading, Writing, and Research in Grades 3–8*. Portland, ME: Stenhouse.

Harvey, Stephanie, and Anne Goudvis. 2007. *Toolkit Texts: Short Nonfiction for Guided and Independent Practice*. Portsmouth, NH: Firsthand/Heinemann.

Heard, Georgia. 1998. *Awakening the Heart: Exploring Poetry in Elementary and Middle School*. Portsmouth, NH: Heinemann.

Hutchins, Pat. 1986. *The Doorbell Rang*. New York: Greenwillow.

Jenkins, Steve. 2009. *Never Smile at a Monkey: And 17 Other Important Things to Remember*. Boston: Houghton Mifflin for Children.

Klein, Abby. 2006. *Shark Tooth Tale*. Ready, Freddy! series. New York: Scholastic.

Kramer, Stephen P. 1995. *Caves*. Minneapolis: Carolrhoda.

Lauber, Patricia. 2000. *The True or False Book About Horses*. New York: HarperCollins.

Levine, Ellen. 1992. *If You Traveled West in a Covered Wagon*. New York: Scholastic.

Liu, Daphne. 2010. "Great Migrations: Move as Millions, Survive as One." *National Geographic Explorer*. November–December: 2–9.

Lusted, Marcia A. 2009a. "Taking a Bath . . . With Friends." *Appleseeds*. September: 13–15.

———. 2009b. "Have a Toga Party!" *Appleseeds*. September: 24–25.

Martin, Jacqueline Briggs. 2009. *Snowflake Bentley*. Boston: Houghton Mifflin Harcourt.

McGovern, Ann. 1990. *The Secret Soldier: The Story of Deborah Sampson*. New York: Scholastic.

Moline, Steve. 2012. *I See What You Mean: Visual Literacy K–8*. 2nd ed. Portland, ME: Stenhouse.

Montgomery, Sy. 2004. *The Tarantula Scientist*. Boston: Houghton Mifflin.

Moss, Barbara. 2004. "Teaching Expository Text Structures Through Informational Trade Book Retellings." *The Reading Teacher* 57 (8): 710–718.

Murray, Donald M. 1978. "Write Before Writing." *College Composition and Communication* 29 (4): 375–381.

Numeroff, Laura Joffe. 1985. *If You Give a Mouse a Cookie*. New York: Harper and Row.

Pallotta, Jerry. 2010. *Polar Bear vs. Grizzly Bear*. Who Would Win? series. New York: Scholastic.

———. 2011. *Komodo Dragon vs. King Cobra*. Who Would Win? series. New York: Scholastic.

Penner, Lucille Recht. 2002. *Liberty! How the Revolutionary War Began.* New York: Random House.

Ray, Katie Wood, and Lester L. Laminack. 2001. *The Writing Workshop: Working Through the Hard Parts (and They're All Hard Parts).* Urbana, IL: National Council of Teachers of English.

Rosswurm, M. A. 2012. "Cheetah and Dog: Best Friends Forever." *Highlights for Children* 67 (7): 28.

Ryan, Pam Muñoz. 1998. *Riding Freedom.* New York: Scholastic.

Schanzer, Rosalyn. 2004. *George vs. George: The American Revolution as Seen from Both Sides.* Washington, DC: National Geographic.

Senior, Kathryn. 2002. *You Wouldn't Want to Be Sick in the 16th Century! Diseases You'd Rather Not Catch.* New York: Franklin Watts.

Settel, Joanne. 1999. *Exploding Ants: Amazing Facts About How Animals Adapt.* New York: Atheneum Books for Young Readers.

Simon, Seymour. 1999. *Tornadoes.* New York: HarperCollins.

Svoboda, Elizabeth. 2012. "How Mosquitoes Survive in a Downpour." *Discover* 33 (2): 13.

Swallow, Pamela Curtis. 2005. *Groundhog Gets a Say.* New York: G. P. Putnam's Sons.

Tavares, Matt. 2012. *There Goes Ted Williams: The Greatest Hitter Who Ever Lived.* Somerville, MA: Candlewick.

Thomas, Don. 2011. "Space Quest." *National Geographic Explorer.* January-February: 16–23.

Thomson, Sarah L. 2006. *Amazing Sharks!* New York: HarperCollins.

Wedner, Diane. 2010. "Far-Out Foods." *National Geographic Explorer.* November-December: 10–15.

Wilder, Laura Ingalls. 2010. *Little House on the Prairie.* 75th anniversary edition. New York: HarperCollins.